Investing for Your Future

A Cooperative Extension System Basic Investing Home Study Course

Written by

Barbara O'Neill
(Project Director)
Rutgers University

Patricia Q. Brennan
Rutgers University

Joyce H. Christenbury
Clemson University

Linda Kirk Fox
University of Idaho

Constance Y. Kratzer
*New Mexico State
University*

Irene Leech
*Virginia Polytechnic Institute
and State University*

Katherine Philipp
U.S. Securities and Exchange Commission

Nancy M. Porter
Clemson University

Jane Schuchardt
*USDA Cooperative State Research,
Education, and Extension Service*

Joan E. Witter
Michigan State University

Natural Resource, Agriculture, and Engineering Service (NRAES)
Cooperative Extension • 152 Riley-Robb Hall • Ithaca, New York 14853-5701

NRAES–156
February 2002

ISBN 0-935817-80-8

Library of Congress Cataloging-in-Publication Data

Investing for your future : a cooperative extension system basic investing home study course / authors, Barbara O'Neill (project director) … [et al.].
    p. cm. -- (NRAES-156)
    Includes bibliographical references.
    ISBN 0-935817-80-8 (pbk.)
    1. Finance, Personal--Handbooks, manuals, etc. 2. Investments--Handbooks, manuals, etc. I. O'Neill, Barbara M. II. Natural Resource, Agriculture, and Engineering Service. Cooperative Extension. III. NRAES (Series) ; 156.

HG179 .I493 2002
332.6--dc21

2001058650

Natural Resource, Agriculture, and Engineering Service (NRAES)
Cooperative Extension • 152 Riley-Robb Hall
Ithaca, New York 14853-5701
Phone: (607) 255-7654 • Fax: (607) 254-8770
E-mail: NRAES@CORNELL.EDU • Web site: WWW.NRAES.ORG

Table of Contents

Dear Home Study Course Reader,

Welcome to the home study course *Investing For Your Future*. This 11-unit home study course was developed by the Cooperative Extension System for beginning investors with small dollar amounts to invest at any one time. It is assumed that many readers will be investing for the first time or selecting investment products, such as a stock index fund or unit investment trust, that they have not purchased previously.

The course units were developed in a logical order. "Basic" topics such as setting goals, investment terms (e.g., diversification, dollar-cost averaging, asset allocation), and finding money to invest lay a foundation to help readers understand how and why they're investing. You'll also begin to understand that there's generally a trade off between risk and reward. The more risk an investor assumes, the greater the chance of a high return, as well as the greater chance of loss.

After exploring "the basics," the course describes specific types of investments (e.g., stocks and bonds) in detail. You'll begin to understand their characteristics, how they are purchased, and what it costs to purchase each investment. There are also units that focus specifically on tax-advantaged investments and investments that can be purchased with less than $1,000.

Finally, *Investing For Your Future* concludes with additional topics of use to investors: available resources, how to select professional financial advisors, and information to help you avoid becoming a victim of investment fraud. You can choose to read the entire course, in any order that makes sense to you, or select only those topics that are of most interest. The choice is yours.

Simply reading *Investing For Your Future* will not turn you into a successful investor, however. A printed page simply can never replace the personal motivation that is required to take action to achieve financial goals. That is why there are "action steps" listed at the end of each unit. These are specific steps that readers can take to apply the course material to their lives. We urge you to consider each action step carefully and take action that is appropriate for your individual financial situation. The course also contains a number of worksheets, which, again, are tools to help readers apply the information contained within each unit.

Another resource to help you achieve your financial goals is your local Cooperative Extension office. Look in the "county government" section of your phone book to find the nearest office. Free or low-cost publications are available, as well as classes, Web sites, computerized financial analyses, newsletters, and other program delivery methods.

Thank you for participating in *Investing For Your Future*. We hope that you find it helpful and that all of your future financial goals are achieved.

About This Home Study Course

This 11-unit home-study course was developed by a consortium of six land-grant universities (Rutgers University, Clemson University, Virginia Tech, Michigan State University, New Mexico State University, and the University of Idaho); the U.S. Department of Agriculture Cooperative State Research, Education, and Extension Service; and the U.S. Securities and Exchange Commission. The course was originally sponsored by Rutgers Cooperative Extension, New Brunswick, New Jersey, with cash and/or in-kind support from participating universities and federal agencies. It was first published in February 2000 by Rutgers Cooperative Extension; New Jersey Agricultural Experiment Station; and Rutgers, The State University of New Jersey.

In 2002, *Investing For Your Future* was reviewed and completely revised to provide current information about investments affected by the 2001 tax law. Partial funding for the course update was provided by the Foundation for Financial Planning, <www.foundation-finplan.org>. The 2002 course was published by the Natural Resource, Agriculture, and Engineering Service (NRAES). For additional research-based personal finance information, consult the Web sites <www.money2000.org> and <www.sec.gov>. For more information about NRAES, visit <www.nraes.org>.

Acknowledgments

Investing For Your Future is the result of hundreds of hours of time devoted by dozens of individuals. Special appreciation is extended to the following people, who assisted with the writing, editing, and reviewing of the course. Several focus groups tested the course before it was initially launched.

Authors
Patricia Q. Brennan, Rutgers University; Joyce H. Christenbury, Clemson University; Linda Kirk Fox, University of Idaho; Constance Y. Kratzer, New Mexico State University; Irene Leech, Virginia Polytechnic Institute and State University; Barbara O'Neill, Rutgers University; Katherine Philipp, U.S. Securities and Exchange Commission; Nancy M. Porter, Clemson University; Jane Schuchardt, U.S. Department of Agriculture; and Joan E. Witter, Michigan State University.

Peer Reviewers
For the original 2000 version: William Bailey, U.S. Department of Agriculture; Claudia Kerbel, University of Rhode Island; Chris Koehler, Washington State University; Alma Owen, Purdue University; Janice Shelton, University of Arizona; and Mary J. Stephenson, University of Maryland.

For the 2002 version: Cheryl Besl, North American Securities Administrators Association; Claudia Kerbel, University of Rhode Island; Constance Y. Kratzer, New Mexico State University; Ruth Lytton, Virginia Polytechnic Institute and State University; Gene Nugent, U.S. Treasury; Barbara O'Neill, Rutgers University; Barbara S. Poole, The American College; Jane Schuchardt, USDA Cooperative State Research, Education, and Extension Service; Elizabeth S. Trent, University of Vermont; and Josephine Turner, University of Florida.

Project Staff
James A. Brennan, ActiveWeb Consulting, Freehold, New Jersey; Beth E. Hazen, Willows End, Cortland, New York; Gary Huntzinger, Manager, Cook College Computing Services; and Cathleen Walker, NRAES (Natural Resource, Agriculture, and Engineering Service).

Washington, DC Consumer Focus Group
Lisa Ghebresill Assie, Connie D. Austin, Carolyn S. Barbarito, Dolores Langford Bridgette, Terri J. Brooker, Gina Davis, Theresa E. Davis, Mi Cha Goewgy, Doris M. Green, Pamela Gussom, Jack Hardy, Mildred L. Harris, Jacqueline Johnson Hayes, Barbara J. Katz, Craig Miller, Sakinah J. Munir, Katherine Philipp, Sylvia Pilkerton, Brenda L. Robbins, Linda Schneider, Jane Schuchardt, Lynne M. Smith, and Diane White.

Roanoke, VA Focus Group with Professional Financial Educators and Counselors
William Bailey, Nancy Bolitho, L. Ann Coulson, Charlotte F. Crawford, Regina Dolan, Constance Y. Kratzer, JoAnn Linck, Ruth Lytton, Joseph A. Onesta, Linda Rady, Gwen Reichbach, Joseph L. Sgarwata, Steven S. Shagrin, and Mary J. Stephenson.

Project Director
Barbara O'Neill, Rutgers University.

Basic Building Blocks OF SUCCESSFUL FINANCIAL MANAGEMENT

Unit 1

Nancy M. Porter, Ph.D., CFCS, Clemson University Cooperative Extension

Investing is an important part of the financial planning process. Yet, information overload and busy lives make managing finances successfully a challenge for almost everyone at some point. This unit is designed to help you understand the basic building blocks of sound financial management–the steps you need to complete, or at least consider, before you begin an investment program. Visualizing the financial management building blocks in a pyramid (figure 1), the wealth protection blocks on the bottom of the pyramid form a strong, secure foundation and provide crucial stability for the wealth accumulation and distribution blocks on top.

Each building block relies upon the strength and stability of the personal finance strategies used in the blocks below it. Decisions for one building block may have a definite impact on options available in adjacent blocks. For example, if you overuse credit, you may not qualify for a mortgage on a home. As you

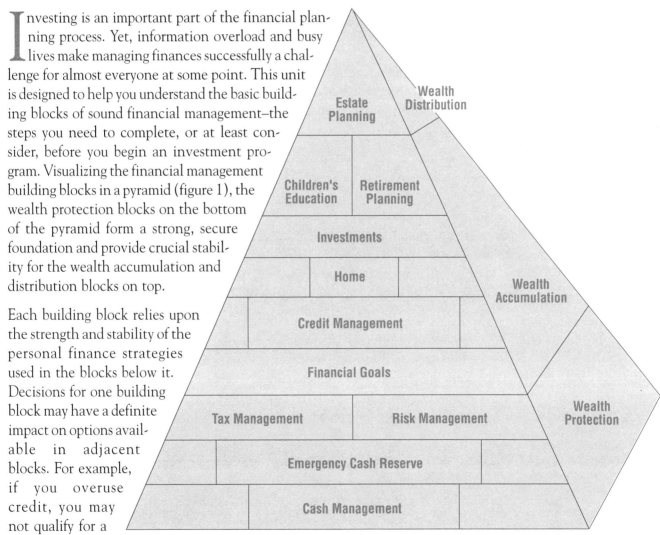

Figure 1. Building Blocks of Financial Management.

move up the pyramid, your financial life becomes more complex. This complexity, along with changes in your life, may require that you reevaluate and change earlier strategies. Working from the bottom to the top of the pyramid, we will discuss the 11 key components of a successful financial plan that make up the blocks of the pyramid. We will discuss in turn the components of wealth protection, accumulation, and distribution.

Notes

Wealth Protection

Cash Management

Cash management strategies include budgeting, keeping financial records, maximizing the interest earned on checking and savings accounts, and regularly preparing financial statements, such as net worth and cash flow. One of the soundest pieces of financial advice is to spend less than you earn. It sounds simple, but if you are not fully aware of how you spend money, you may be spending more than you realize (see Spending Plan <www.money2000.org>). After you track your income and expenses, following a budget that is adjusted to your individual situation and goals is an excellent strategy to plan your spending (see Interactive Budget <www.money2000.org>).

To estimate the value of your assets and chart your financial progress, each year you should add together everything you own (assets), then subtract everything you owe (debts), including your mortgage and credit card debt. This summary of assets and debts is called a **net worth statement** or **balance sheet**. It will help you analyze the way you currently manage your finances and make decisions to improve your financial situation.

You want your net worth to increase each year. During the early stages of your life, when you're establishing yourself at work and accumulating the necessities of life, your net worth may rise slowly. It will probably grow the most right before retirement when you are at the peak of your career and accumulating assets to ensure a secure retirement. Plan to review and update your net worth annually. The actual date of your review is not important. It might be your birthday, New Year's, right after you do your taxes, or some other important date. It is more important that you remember the date and complete your annual checkup. It also is important to regularly reconcile bank and other financial statements with your own records.

A vital aspect of the cash management building block is financial record-keeping. An effective record-keeping system should be convenient and not too complicated to maintain. A number of systems are available commercially, or you can design your own (e.g., with file folders). It is important that the system makes sense to you and that you use it consistently.

Emergency Cash Reserve

Setting aside money to meet unexpected expenses provides a financial safety net and allows you to take advantage of financial opportunities as they arise. Most experts recommend an **emergency fund** equal to three to six months' living expenses; however, you do not need to set aside this total amount in a low-yielding passbook, certificate of deposit, or money market account. The amount of your emergency fund depends upon your age, health, job outlook, and personal financial situation (e.g., amount and kind of insurance coverage). An emergency fund might be adequate with enough to cover three to six months of expenses using a combination of cash and credit if you have a source of low-cost borrowing (e.g., home equity

credit-line loan, cash-value life insurance, or retirement plan). If your household has multiple sources of income or dual earners, you can count on those other sources of income in an emergency.

You might want a larger emergency fund if you are in business for yourself, your work is seasonal, your job is uncertain, or you rely heavily on commissions. If your health is questionable (e.g., you foresee long-term disability or extensive medical expenses), you anticipate a large expenditure for the care of a relative in the near future, or your child is about to enter college, you may also need a larger cash reserve.

Your emergency cash reserve can be subdivided to minimize penalties for early withdrawal of large amounts of funds at one time and to maximize interest earned on accounts should an emergency occur. Money that would be needed within three months of a financial emergency is best placed in an interest-bearing checking account, passbook savings, money-market deposit account, money market mutual fund, or short-term certificates of deposit (CDs). Funds needed four to six months after an emergency could be placed in short-term CDs as well as three- and six-month Treasury bills. Money that would not be needed for seven months to two years could be placed in a money market mutual fund and longer term CDs (12-, 18-, and 24-month). Money you can avoid withdrawing for two to five years during a financial emergency could be placed in Treasury notes, short-term bond funds, or three- to five-year CDs.

Risk Management

Every day we are exposed to many risks that can cause a financial loss. Accidents, property damage, illness, and death are risks we often consider. However, other risks, such as the possibility of being sued or becoming disabled and unable to work, are also important. We each have to decide how we will protect ourselves should a risk become a reality. If you do not have a plan, you might have to go into debt or use funds set aside for other financial goals in the event of financial disaster.

Appropriate risk management strategies protect against catastrophic financial losses, regardless of the cause. Good comprehensive insurance coverage against severe setbacks is essential. Areas for coverage include life, health, homeowner's or renter's, auto, disability, and liability. Smart consumers can obtain this coverage at a cost that allows them to move up the pyramid to accomplish other goals without being insurance poor. Note that this type of risk management should not be confused with investment risk, which is a different financial concept.

To determine when you need to purchase insurance, consider the best way to handle each of your risks. Because your risks change over a lifetime, evaluate your situation every few years and make appropriate changes. Can your savings cover a financial loss so that you don't need to buy insurance? Increasing the deductibles (the portion of a loss that you pay) on your policy usually saves you money as well. However, when self-insuring or carrying high deductibles on policies, you must set aside the necessary funds in your emergency cash reserve to pay for those expenses in case of a loss.

Risk management strategies can be combined with savings and investments to achieve financial goals (e.g., buying cash value life insurance). However, be careful to ensure that your strategies provide the best return on the money involved. Determine if insurance protection can be purchased less expensively so that you can invest the savings for a greater overall return.

Tax Management

The goal for taxpayers is to pay no more than the least possible tax owed. Avoiding taxes through legal tax strategies is not to be confused with illegal tax evasion. Legally avoiding taxes means using effective financial record-keeping, decision making, and planning strategies to reduce your total income tax . One example of good tax management is adjusting the amount of federal income tax withheld from your paycheck. If you receive a big income tax refund (over $500) each year, you are giving the federal government an interest-free loan. Evaluate the amount you have withheld and determine if you could use this money more effectively throughout the year to manage cash flow or invest for financial goals.

Tax laws continue to dictate how we structure our financial plans. As laws favor or disallow certain strategies, we need to make adjustments. Two examples of this phenomenon are Individual Retirement Accounts (IRAs) and home equity credit-line loans. When everyone was allowed a tax deduction for a traditional IRA, this strategy was widely encouraged and used. Since tax laws restricted IRA deductions, many people automatically either turn to Roth IRAs or eliminate IRAs completely as a viable alternative. Now that tax deductions for nonmortgage consumer interest are not allowed, many people have turned to home equity credit-line loans to finance large purchases and deduct the resulting interest.

As tax laws change, adjust your financial plans to use strategies that are most favorable to your situation. Most of us are aware of the tax advantages of tax-deferred savings. The idea, of course, is to put off paying income taxes on money until you withdraw it in retirement when, possibly, your tax bracket may be lower. However, you have no guarantee that this will happen, especially if you are very successful at saving for retirement and accumulating assets. In addition, the tax laws are constantly changing. You should seek the advice of a Certified Public Accountant (CPA), Certified Financial Planner (CFP), or tax professional to gain insight into how tax laws will affect you.

For example, under a tax law effective May 7, 1997, up to $250,000 of profit from the sale of a primary residence is tax-free if you file an individual tax return; up to $500,000 if you and your spouse file jointly. To qualify for this tax-free benefit, you must own and live in your home for two of the five years prior to the sale. Only one spouse is required to own the home, but both need to have lived there to qualify for the larger $500,000 capital-gain tax exclusion. Further, you can use this new exclusion even if you have previously claimed the old $125,000 exclusion. How often you use this new exclusion is unlimited, but generally you can qualify only once in any two-year period. If you must sell a home because of ill health, a job-related

Notes

move, or unforeseen circumstances prior to meeting the two-year test, you can claim a prorated exclusion (see Internal Revenue Service <www.irs.gov>).

Wealth Accumulation

Financial Goals

To get where you want to go in life, it is important to decide in advance how you will get there. Goals are signposts on the highway to the future. They serve as your guide to personal, career, and financial success. By keeping specific goals in view, you can direct your energies toward achieving your goals.

Financial goals are important, because they help us to organize and direct our financial lives, providing a framework for decision-making. They can help us cope, provide some control in an environment where many things seem out of control, and help us visualize our financial future (see Goal Setting <www.money2000.org>).

How can you establish financial goals and utilize the building blocks you need to achieve your dreams? First, you can learn how to create $MART goals. $MART financial goals have several important criteria:

$	Must be SPECIFIC with dollar amounts, dates, and resources to be used in accomplishing the goals.
M	Must be MEASURABLE; determine regular amounts weekly, bimonthly, or monthly to set aside to accomplish goals. Another good "M" word to consider is MUTUAL. Goals that are mutual or shared with other family members will be easier to achieve. It also is important to think about how you will keep yourself and other family members MOTIVATED to achieve goals, especially long-term goals.
A	Your goals need to be ATTAINABLE given your financial situation.
R	It is important that your goals are RELEVANT and REALISTIC. What RESOURCES are available for you to use in achieving your goals? It is also important that you REVIEW and REVISE your goals periodically as necessary.
T	You need a specific TIME-LINE for accomplishing your goals. To achieve those goals, you must also be willing to make TRADE-OFFS in your financial life. Know the difference between needs and wants. Because there is never enough money to fund all of your financial goals at one time, you need to prioritize your goals.

Take the time to put your goals in writing. Putting them on paper will reinforce their significance. Use the worksheet "$MART Financial Goal-Setting" on page 9 to help you list short- and long-term financial goals. Then, to stay motivated, visualize how you will feel when you accomplish your goals. Lastly, it is very important that you periodically set aside a predetermined sum of money for each specific financial goal (see Saving More <www.money2000.org>).

Notes

Credit Management

When is the best time to stop a growing debt burden? Before it gets out of hand, of course. You can spot a debt problem early by looking at indicators, such as the number of bills coming in each month. Is the number increasing steadily? This could signal an increasing reliance on the use of credit. Cut back on credit buying now; you will be ahead of the game. Are you consistently paying only the minimum each month on your credit cards or other debts? This habit can be a critical "red flag." If you can pay only the minimum now, do not increase your debt load. Also, keep in mind that, when you pay only the minimum amount each month, you are paying high finance charges on the unpaid balance. This costs money and delays the achievement of financial goals.

Periodically, get a copy of your credit report and check it for accuracy and completeness. This is especially important before making large purchases where you plan to use credit, such as for a car loan or a mortgage. In many cases credit reports have minor inaccuracies that need to be corrected. Sometimes there are errors that might result in your being turned down for a loan (to correct an incorrect credit report, use the form provided by the credit reporting agency). Contact *Equifax* (1-800-685-1111, <www.equifax.com>), *Experian* (1-888-397-3742, <www.experian.com>), or *Trans Union* (1-800-916-8800, <www.tuc.com>) for details. If you have recently been denied credit, employment, insurance, or rental housing based on information contained in your credit report, you are entitled to a copy free of charge from the company that issued the report on which the credit denial was based. You can also check your credit score online at <www.myfico.com>, <www.equifax.com>, and <www.eloan.com>.

> **Credit management strategies can be used to:**
> ✓ Avoid the overuse of credit
> ✓ Lower the total amount of debt
> ✓ Shorten the term of debt
> ✓ Reduce interest and finance charges paid for the use of credit

If you have large credit card balances, it is a good idea to repay them before starting an investment plan. Repaying your debts can often provide a greater return on monies than most investment strategies. Repaying high-interest-rate loans can also provide money that can be used for future investments (see Reducing Debt <www.money2000.org>).

Home Ownership

Home ownership is a financial goal for many people. A home is often the largest investment, and sometimes the only investment, that many people make. Given the low appreciation rate of real estate in some areas, it is probably better to think of purchasing a home as buying shelter, not as an investment that you expect to rapidly appreciate (increase in value). Home equity, the dollar value of a home in excess of the mortgage owed on it, is considered an asset against which you can borrow. This strategy must be used with extreme caution, however; you could lose your home if you do not repay the amount borrowed.

Investments

You don't have to be a big-time, high-income investor to have an investment plan. Even if you have only a small savings account, investments can become part of a long-term strategy to achieve specific goals.

A diversified investment portfolio can be developed after building the blocks of a firm financial foundation. Until adequate cash management, an emergency fund, insurance plans, tax management, and credit usage are under control and functioning effectively, it is probably unwise to begin an aggressive investment program.

A diversified investment plan begins with a well-defined philosophy and encompasses strategies designed to specifically accomplish financial goals (e.g., children's education and funding retirement) without having to sacrifice one goal for the other (see Building Wealth and Investing Wisely <www.money2000.org>).

Children's Education

Are you planning to provide your child or children with a college education? If so, do you know how much it will cost? Do you know how you will finance this goal?

Meeting the financial costs of educating children is a financial goal for many people. The strategies to help you meet this goal may differ from other saving and investment strategies, however. Always investigate the tax and financial aid implications of your college-saving strategies.

The earlier you start planning for a college education for your child, the more time you will have to accumulate funds. Consider and plan for the cost of the entire college education. However, because saving ahead for the total cost may be unrealistic for parents, other possibilities need to be explored, including scholarships, grants, loans, and work-study programs. Learn the details about each one.

Retirement Planning

Planning for retirement is a challenge for everyone. Again, the earlier you begin, the longer you will have to accumulate funds and capitalize on compound interest. A plan designed to meet specific retirement goals may be separate from or part of the investment building block.

Some people have given a great deal of thought to retirement. About 46% of working Americans have made a retirement savings calculation, according to the 2001 Retirement Confidence Survey. Seventy-one percent of Americans have already begun to save for retirement. Unfortunately, this means that almost one-third have not yet begun saving. Most experts believe that regular, systematic savings is a habit that is best established early and maintained not only throughout the working years, but into the early stages of retirement since people are living much longer. Today, many people spend as many years in retirement as they spent in the workforce.

Financial experts have long described sources of retirement income as the three-

Notes

legged stool: Social Security, company pension, and personal savings. Now with the growing concern over the future of Social Security, the reduction in benefits offered by employers, and the low personal savings rate, many see the three legs of the retirement income stool becoming shaky. Many say that the stool may need a fourth leg—paid work after retirement.

Now that the Social Security Administration has phased in automatic mailing of Personal Earnings and Benefit Estimate Statements to all wage earners, check yours for accuracy. It contains information that provides an excellent basis for retirement planning. Contact the Social Security Administration (1-800-772-1213; see Social Security online at <www.ssa.gov>) to obtain a benefit request form.

Another source of retirement information is your employer's personnel department which may have general tips on retirement as well as specific information about investments available in your pension plan. Many online sites provide information about retirement planning (see American Savings Education Council <www.asec.org>).

Wealth Distribution

Estate Planning

If you successfully implement the strategies outlined in the financial management pyramid, you are much more likely to have assets left over at the end of your lifetime and will need a plan for how your accumulated wealth is to be distributed. A will is a necessity if you want to direct the distribution of possessions after death. Yet, almost 70% of the adults in the United States do not have wills. Many people think they do not need to prepare a will because they have so little, or it costs too much, or they will do it later when they have more time or get older. Dying without a will is called dying "intestate" and means that state regulations will determine the distribution of assets. By having a carefully written legal will, you can provide for your family and others in a manner consistent with your desires.

In addition, a variety of other important legal documents can make provisions for crises other than your death including the following: General Durable Power of Attorney, Health Care Power of Attorney, and a Living Will. These documents are best completed before a crisis occurs and can ease a difficult period for your family. These components of an estate plan are not directly linked to the financial management pyramid, but can protect assets and ensure that your financial strategies and health care decisions are respected.

Summary

All the building blocks of successful financial management, including investing, are interrelated. Strategies used in one part of the pyramid can directly impact others. If one building block, such as credit use, becomes too large, the entire pyramid can topple. This pyramid aids effective decision making and the successful achievement of financial goals, because all aspects of your financial situation are considered simultaneously.

Worksheet: $MART Financial Goal-Setting

$MART goals need to be written down on paper to reinforce their importance. Use the worksheet at the right to set some short- and long-term financial goals that follow the $MART goal format.

To get where you want to go in life, decide in advance how you will get there. Goals are signposts on the highway to the future. They serve as your road map to personal, career, and financial success. By keeping specific goals in view, you can direct your energies toward achieving your goals.

SHORT-TERM GOALS (LESS THAN ONE YEAR)

GOAL	TOTAL COST	TARGET DATE	AMOUNT TO SAVE/MONTH

LONG-TERM GOALS (LONGER THAN ONE YEAR)

GOAL	TOTAL COST	TARGET DATE	AMOUNT TO SAVE/MONTH

Remember Your $mart Goals

$ $pecific

M Measurable, Mutual, Motivated

A Attainable

R Relevant, Realistic, Resources, Review, Revise

T Time-Line, Trade-Offs

Action Steps

✔ **Take action now.**
Basic Building Blocks of
Successful Financial Management

Check off the steps after you have completed them.

Cash Management

❑ Develop financial management knowledge and skills, i.e., record-keeping, budgeting, tax, risk, and credit management.

❑ Reduce expenditures to free up money to help achieve financial goals.

❑ Compare financial account statements provided by institutions with personal records.

❑ Complete an annual financial checkup, including net worth and cash flow statements.

❑ Build a team of financial advisors to guide and direct financial decision making.

❑ Review financial management strategies periodically and revise when necessary.

Emergency Cash Reserve

❑ Determine/establish adequate amount of emergency fund for your individual situation.

❑ Deposit funds in easily available accounts where they can be accessed with minimal financial penalties.

Risk Management

❑ Locate your insurance policies such as life, health, property, casualty, automobile, and disability.

❑ Evaluate current policies and shop around for additional or replacement coverage if indicated.

Tax Management

❑ Learn about tax laws and use related strategies to reduce total taxes owed.

❑ Check your income tax withholding level and adjust, if indicated. Explore the advantages of different tax strategies.

❑ Utilize tax-advantaged and tax-deferred options when appropriate, i.e., IRAs, 401(k), 403(b).

❑ Maximize tax deductions (e.g., using home equity credit-line loans versus nondeductible consumer interest).

Financial Goals

❑ Write out short-, medium-, and long-term financial goals following the $MART goal format.

Credit Management

❑ Keep credit use at a safe, manageable level.

❑ Obtain a copy of your credit report to see if it is accurate and complete.

Home Ownership/Investments/Children's Education/ Retirement Planning

❑ Determine which of these categories contain areas you wish to include in your financial goals.

❑ Write down specific financial goals for those categories following the $MART goal format.

Estate Planning

❑ Establish and periodically evaluate wills and estate plans.

References

Financial Literacy Center. (1997, January/February). Emergency fund pyramid. *Loose Change Newsletter*, 4.

Porter, N. M., & Christenbury, J. H. (1997, January). *Money 2000 program notebook* (Clemson University Cooperative Extension Service). Clemson, SC: Family and Youth Development Department.

Quinn, J. B. (1998, July 26). Calculating a target for retirement savings. *The Washington Post*, H2.

The 2001 retirement confidence survey summary of findings (2001). Washington, DC: Employee Benefit Research Institute.

Tritch, T. (1997, May). You're never too young to get your estate in shape. *Money*, 91–95.

Author Profile

Nancy M. Porter, Ph.D., is a Professor and Family Resource Management Specialist with the Clemson University Cooperative Extension Service <fyd.clemson.edu/porter.htm>. Her primary areas of expertise are family financial management and consumer education. Prior to joining the faculty at Clemson, Dr. Porter taught at Delta State University in Mississippi and in the Towanda Area Public Schools in Pennsylvania. Dr. Porter completed her B.S. and M.S. in Home Economics Education at Mansfield University in Pennsylvania. Her Ph.D. in Family Resource Management was earned at Virginia Tech.

Inve$ting Basics

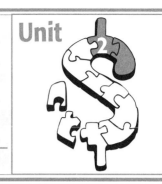

— Joan E. Witter, M.S., Michigan State University Extension —

In Unit 1, you learned about financial building blocks such as cash management. Now it's time to examine basic investing principles. Wise investing requires knowledge of key financial concepts and an understanding of your personal investment profile and how these work together to impact investing decisions.

This unit will:

✦ Discuss the difference between saving and investing

✦ Illustrate the risk/rate-of-return tradeoff

✦ Explain the importance of the time-value of money and asset allocation

✦ Challenge you to think about your personal risk tolerance

✦ Help you to recognize that your tax bracket, financial goals, and time horizon are key factors in defining an appropriate investment plan and asset mix for you and your family

The Difference Between Saving and Investing

Even though the words "saving" and "investing" are often used interchangeably, there are differences between the two.

Saving provides funds for emergencies and for making specific purchases in the relatively near future (usually three years or less). Safety of the principal and liquidity of the funds (ease of converting to cash) are important aspects of savings dollars. Because of these characteristics, savings dollars generally yield a low rate of return and do not maintain purchasing power.

Savings $$ ✦	Investment $$
Safe ✦	Involve risk
Easily accessible ✦	Volatile in short time periods
Low return ✦	Offer potential appreciation
Used for short-term goals ✦	Used for mid- and long-term goals

Investing, on the other hand, focuses on increasing net worth and achieving long-term financial goals. Investing involves risk (of loss of principal) and is to be considered only after you have adequate savings.

Investment Return

Total return is the profit (or loss) on an investment. It is a combination of current income (cash received from interest, dividends, etc.) and capital gains or losses (the change in value of the investment between the time you bought and sold it). The published **rate of return** for a selected investment is usually expressed as a percentage of the current price on an annual basis. However, the **real rate of return** is the rate of return earned after inflation, which is further reduced by income taxes and transaction costs.

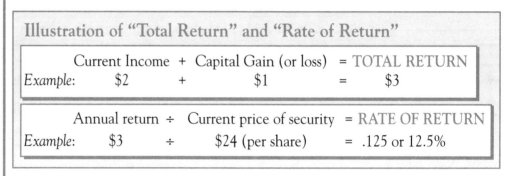

The average annual rates of return for the major investment asset classes from 1926–2000, according to the Chicago investment research firm, Ibbotson Associates, are shown in figure 1.

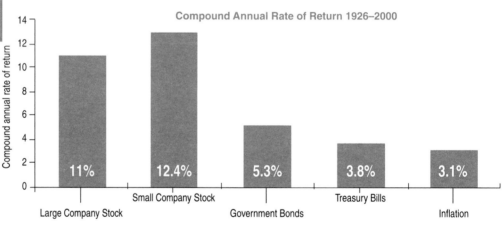

Figure 1. Compound Annual Rate of Return.
Source: Ibbotson Associates, 2001

Risk

ALL investments involve some **risk**, because the future value of an investment is never certain. Risk, simply stated, is the possibility that the ACTUAL return on an investment will vary from the EXPECTED return or that the initial principal will decline in value. Risk implies the possibility of loss on your investment.

Factors that affect the risk level of an investment include:

> ✦ Inflation
> ✦ Business failure
> ✦ Changes in the economy
> ✦ Interest rate changes

The Risk / Rate-of-Return Relationship

Generally speaking, risk and rate of return are directly related. As the risk level of an investment increases, the potential return usually increases as well. The pyramid of investment risk (figure 2) illustrates the risk and return associated with various types of investment options. As investors move up the pyramid, they incur a greater risk of loss of principal along with the potential for higher returns.

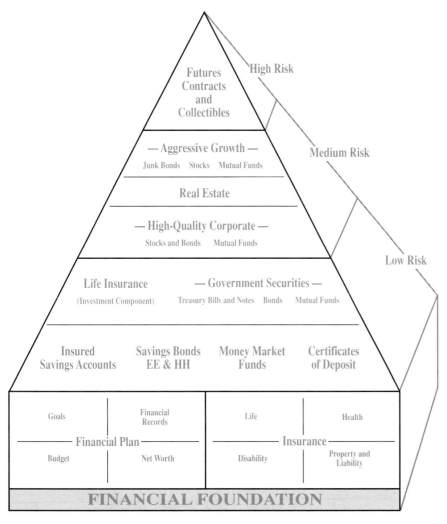

Figure 2. Pyramid of Investment Risk.
Source: National Institute for Consumer Education, 1998

Diversification

You can do several things to offset the impact of some types of risk. Diversifying your investment portfolio by selecting a variety of securities is one frequently used strategy. Done properly, diversification can reduce about 70% of the total risk of investing. Think about it. If you put all of your money in one place, your return will depend solely on the performance of that one investment. Alternatively, if you invest in several assets, your return will depend on an average of your various investment returns. Here are three basic ways to diversify your investments:

- ✦ By choosing securities from a **variety of asset classes**, e.g., a mix of stock, bonds, cash, and real estate
- ✦ By choosing a variety of securities or funds **within one asset class**, e.g., stocks from large, medium, small, and international companies in different industries
- ✦ By choosing a **variety of maturity dates** for fixed-income (bond) investments

By diversifying, you won't lose as much as if you invested in just one security right before its market value goes down. However, if the market goes straight up from the time you started, you won't make as much in a diversified portfolio, either. However, historically, most people are concerned about protection from dramatic losses.

Dollar-Cost Averaging

Another technique to help soften the impact of fluctuations in the investment market is **dollar-cost averaging**. You invest a set amount of money on a regular basis over a long period of time—regardless of the price per share of the investment. In doing so, you purchase more shares when the price per share is down and fewer shares when the market is high. As a result, you will acquire most of the shares at a below-average cost per share.

Look at the dollar-cost averaging illustration below. One hundred dollars is invested each month. Due to fluctuations in the market, the number of shares purchased with the $100 each month varies, because the shares vary in price from $5 to $10. You can see that, when the share price is down, you acquire more shares as in months 2, 3, and 4. You benefit when/if the price per share goes up.

	Regular Investment	Share Price	Shares Acquired
Month 1	$100	$10.00	10.0
Month 2	100	7.50	13.3
Month 3	100	5.00	20.0
Month 4	100	7.50	13.3
Month 5	100	10.00	10.0
Total	$500	$40.00	66.6
Your Average Share Cost: $500 ÷ 66.6 = $7.50			

Figure 3. Dollar-Cost Averaging Illustration

As most investors know, market timing…always buying low and selling high…is very hard to accomplish. Dollar-cost averaging takes much of the emotion and guesswork out of investing. Profits will accelerate when investment market prices rise. At the same time, losses will be limited during times of declining prices. For most people, dollar-cost averaging is not so much a way of making extra money as a way to limit risk.

The Time-Value of Money

Now that you understand the concepts of risk and return, let's turn to an element that is at the heart and soul of building wealth and financial security…**TIME**.

Here is how time can work for you:

1. The longer you invest, the more money you will accumulate.

2. The more money you invest, the more it will accumulate because of the magic of compound interest.

Compounding works like this....

The interest earned on your investments is reinvested or left on deposit. At the next calculation, interest is earned on the original principal PLUS the reinvested interest. Earning interest on accumulated interest over time generates more and more money.

COMPOUND INTEREST
Interest credited daily, monthly, quarterly, semiannually, or annually on both principal and previously credited interest.

Compounding also applies to dividends and capital gains on investments when they are reinvested. The following illustration and questions give you a firsthand opportunity to calculate the impact of time on the value of your investment accumulation. Please complete the exercise on the next page before moving ahead to the next section.

Exercise: How Time Affects the Value of Money

Investor A invests $2,000 a year for ten years, beginning at age 25. Investor B waits ten years, then invests $2,000 a year for 31 years. Compare the total contributions and the total value at retirement of the two investments. This example assumes a 9% fixed rate of return, compounded monthly. All interest is left in the account to allow interest to be earned on interest.

Investor A				Investor B			
Age	Years	Contributions	Year End Value	Age	Years	Contributions	Year End Value
25	1	$ 2,000	$2,188	25	1	$ 0	$ 0
26	2	2,000	4,580	26	2	0	0
27	3	2,000	7,198	27	3	0	0
28	4	2,000	10,061	28	4	0	0
29	5	2,000	13,192	29	5	0	0
30	6	2,000	16,617	30	6	0	0
31	7	2,000	20,363	31	7	0	0
32	8	2,000	24,461	32	8	0	0
33	9	2,000	28,944	33	9	0	0
34	10	2,000	33,846	34	10	0	0
35	11	0	37,021	35	11	2,000	2,188
36	12	0	40,494	36	12	2,000	4,580
37	13	0	44,293	37	13	2,000	7,198
38	14	0	48,448	38	14	2,000	10,061
39	15	0	52,992	39	15	2,000	13,192
40	16	0	57,963	40	16	2,000	16,617
41	17	0	63,401	41	17	2,000	20,363
42	18	0	69,348	42	18	2,000	24,461
43	19	0	75,854	43	19	2,000	28,944
44	20	0	82,969	44	20	2,000	33,846
45	21	0	90,752	45	21	2,000	39,209
46	22	0	99,265	46	22	2,000	45,075
47	23	0	108,577	47	23	2,000	51,490
48	24	0	118,763	48	24	2,000	58,508
49	25	0	129,903	49	25	2,000	66,184
50	26	0	142,089	50	26	2,000	74,580
51	27	0	155,418	51	27	2,000	83,764
52	28	0	169,997	52	28	2,000	93,809
53	29	0	185,944	53	29	2,000	104,797
54	30	0	203,387	54	30	2,000	116,815
55	31	0	222,466	55	31	2,000	129,961
56	32	0	243,335	56	32	2,000	144,340
57	33	0	266,162	57	33	2,000	160,068
58	34	0	291,129	58	34	2,000	177,271
59	35	0	318,439	59	35	2,000	196,088
60	36	0	348,311	60	36	2,000	216,670
61	37	0	380,985	61	37	2,000	239,182
62	38	0	416,724	62	38	2,000	263,807
63	39	0	455,816	63	39	2,000	290,741
64	40	0	498,574	64	40	2,000	320,202
65	41	0	545,344	65	41	2,000	352,427
Value at Retirement			$545,344	Value at Retirement			$352,427
Less Total Contributions			$20,000	Less Total Contributions			$62,000
Net Earnings			$525,344	Net Earnings			$290,427

Source: National Institute for Consumer Education, 1998

Using the data for investors A & B, answer the following questions:

1. At $2,000 a year, how much did Investor A invest in the ten years between the ages of 25 and 35?

_____

2. What is the value of Investor A's investment when the Investor is 35?

_____

3. At $2,000 a year, how much did Investor B invest over the 31 years, from age 35 through 65?

_____

4. What is the value at retirement of Investor A's investment?

_____

5. What is the value at retirement of Investor B's investment?

_____

6. What are Investor A's net earnings?

_____

7. What are Investor B's net earnings?

_____

8. What advice would you give to your children about investing for their retirement?

_____

_____

_____

_____

Note that Investor A, who invested much less than Investor B, has a much higher nest egg at retirement age, because of a ten-year head start. As you can see from this example, compound interest is especially magical when money is steadily invested and left to grow over a long period.

Answers: 1. 20,000, 2. 37,021, 3. 62,000, 4. 545,344, 5. 352,427, 6. 525,344, 7. 290,427

Asset Allocation

In the final analysis, your overall investment return will be closely associated with the asset categories and allocations that you select. An investor's group of investments, frequently called an investment portfolio, can be divided in numerous ways among stocks, bonds, and cash management options. You might choose a 20/40/40 portfolio—20% stocks, 40% bonds, and 40% cash options—or a 75/20/5 ratio—75% stocks, 20% bonds, and 5% cash.

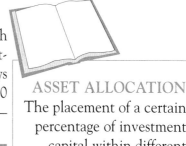

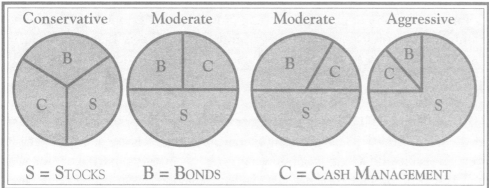

Figure 4. Asset Allocation Options.

Several factors will impact the exact rate of return that you receive on your investment portfolio. Studies show that the most important one, asset allocation, will account for about 90% of your return. The selection of individual securities and market timing will account for the remaining 10% or so. The critical question, of course, is: "What is the ideal asset allocation for you?" Here are several factors to consider as you make this decision.

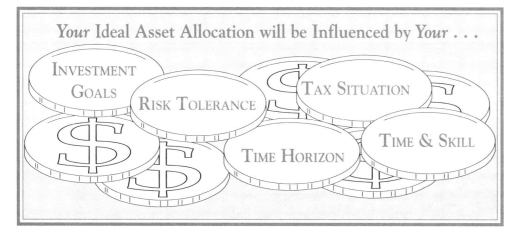

Your Investment Goals

Goals are specific things (e.g., buy a car) that people want to do with their money. As discussed in Unit 1, as people move through various life stages, their needs and financial goals change. Your selection of investments should relate closely to your financial goals; each goal will define the amount and liquidity of the money needed as well as the number of years available for the investment to grow.

Your Risk Tolerance

Risk tolerance is a person's emotional and financial capacity to ride out the ups and downs of the investment market without panicking when the value of investments goes down. Risk tolerances vary widely. Some are associated with personality factors, while others are based on changing needs dictated by your stage in the life cycle. If you won't sleep well at night when the principal value of your investment goes down, you should select saving and investment options with lower risk. On the other hand, it's important to realize that investments that guarantee the safety of principal will not grow your money quickly and may not maintain purchasing power in times of inflation or over a long time span. In reality it's necessary to take some risk just to maintain purchasing power. The question is: "What kind of risks are you willing to take?"

Your Time Horizon

As discussed earlier, *time* is a very important resource to investors. For example, young investors with a long time horizon may choose investments that exhibit wide price swings, knowing that time is available for fluctuations to average out. Families investing for a specific mid-life goal (e.g., funding a child's education or purchasing a home) may choose a more moderate course that has opportunity for growth, but provides more safety for the principal. Individuals nearing retirement and those with the need to depend on investment income to cover daily expenses may wish to select investments that lock in gains and provide a guaranteed income stream.

Your Tax Situation

The return on any investment is influenced by your federal, state, and local tax situation. Investment earnings may be:

> ★ TAXABLE Taxes paid yearly on interest, dividends, and annual capital gain distributions from investments.
> ★ TAX-DEFERRED Taxes on earnings are deferred until withdrawal. Tax-deferred earnings include contributions and returns associated with IRAs, 401(k)s, and other retirement saving plans (see Unit 7).
> ★ TAX-EXEMPT Earnings are wholly or partly free from taxes. Roth IRAs and most municipal bonds are common examples. (Tax-exempt status may be different at the state and federal levels.)

Before selecting an investment, learn its tax consequences for you. Remember, what counts is not what you make on an investment, but **what you get to keep** both now and in the long run.

Time and Skill to Manage Your Portfolio ------------------------------

Some investments require little or no time commitment or special knowledge. Others, such as rental property or a portfolio of high-risk individual stocks, may require constant monitoring and management. How much time are you willing and able to spend?

In a nutshell, the asset allocation that you select must be customized to your situation, needs, and temperament. Spend a few minutes completing the "What are Your Investment Preferences" exercise to help you further clarify and summarize your investing preferences.

What Are Your Investment Preferences?

Consider each pair of words below as a continuum. Place an "x" on each line of the continuum to indicate how important each of these features is to you. Marking the middle of a line would therefore mean that the features were of equal importance. If others are sharing investment responsibility with you, ask them to complete it as well.

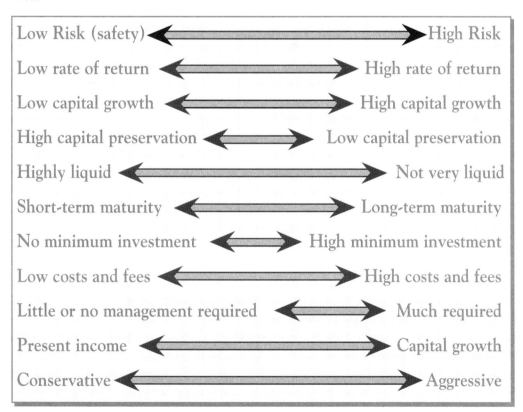

Figure 5. What are Your Investment Preferences?
Adapted from: Hogarth, Jeanne and Swanson, Josephine (1987). TOPICs, Investment Basics, Cornell University, 1987.

Notes

♦ Review your responses carefully.

♦ Check for inconsistences in the preferences you have indicated.
  (For example, do you prefer things that are unlikely to come together,
  e.g., low risk and high return?)

♦ Work to understand and resolve inconsistencies and differences in order to
  assure that your overall investment strategies and asset allocation are consistent with both your needs and your preferences.

Summary

In this unit we have discussed basic financial concepts that you need to understand before becoming involved in an investing program. You've learned about the difference between saving and investing, the predictable tradeoff between risk and return, the importance of time to an investment program, and asset allocation. In addition, you looked at various aspects of your personal situation and their possible impact on your asset allocation decisions.

The steps below suggest important actions for you to take to establish a solid foundation for future investing activity. Once completed, you will be ready to begin developing a personal investment plan. A necessary part of the plan is locating dollars to invest. The next unit will help you meet that challenge.

Action Steps

✔ Take action now.
Investing Basics

Check off the steps after you have completed them.

❑ Review your current financial holdings and determine if they are in saving or investment vehicles.

❑ Determine the rate of return for your current financial holdings.

❑ Establish short-, medium-, and long-term financial goals for you and your family. Estimate the length of time between now and when you want to achieve each goal.

❑ Complete the "What are Your Investment Preferences?" exercise to identify your characteristics and needs as an investor.

❑ Set aside time each week to read one of the family financial magazines recommended in Unit 9.

❑ Assess your interest, skill, and time to make decisions about your investment plan and portfolio. Proceed on your own or seek assistance.

References

2000 Yearbook (2001). Chicago: Ibbotson & Associates.

Consumer approach to investing (1998). Ypsilanti, MI: National Institute for Consumer Education.

Garman, E. T. & Forgue, R. E. (2000). *Personal finance.* 6th Edition. Boston: Houghton Mifflin Company.

Quinn, J. B. (1997). *Making the most of your money.* New York: Simon & Schuster.

Author Profile

Joan Witter worked on the Cooperative Extension staff at Michigan State University for over 20 years. She received both B.S. and M.S. degrees from Michigan State University and is currently Program Leader Emeritus, Extension Family Resource Management Programs.

Finding Money
TO INVEST

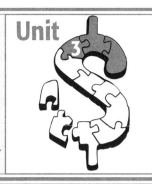

——— Joyce H. Christenbury, M.Ed., CFCS, Clemson University Cooperative Extension———

In Units 1 and 2, you learned about building blocks for financial success and basic investment principles. Next we will explore ways to "find" money for investing. Many Americans are going broke on some of the highest incomes our country has ever seen. Studies estimate that 70% of Americans live from "paycheck to paycheck," courting financial disaster if their income is suddenly reduced or stopped. Generally, Americans are not saving for a "rainy" day; they are consuming it all today. The individual savings rate in the United States fell from 6% to –0.1% of disposable income in the 20-year period from 1980 to 2000.

Are You Satisfied with the Amount You Save?

This unit is designed to help you "find" money to fund your investment plans. We will suggest tools for success, but you have to supply the desire, self-discipline, wise decisions, and good planning to be successful.

Review your financial status by answering these questions:

> ☞ Do I have three to six months' income in an emergency fund?
>
> ☞ Do I save regularly?
>
> ☞ Do I know how much I need to save to achieve future goals?
>
> ☞ Do I save to purchase big-ticket items instead of buying on credit?
>
> ☞ When I use credit, do I save to make as large a down payment as possible?
>
> ☞ Do I save at least 10% of my personal disposable income?
>
> ☞ Do I know how much I need to save for retirement?

The more times you answer "yes" to these questions, the more likely you are a prudent saver. A "no" can help you identify areas where you could do better. Once you have a sound savings program in place, you are ready to invest surplus funds. Unfortunately, many people feel their savings are not sufficient, and they see no way to meet their immediate needs and have extra funds to invest.

Notes

Through this unit of study, you will explore strategies that will help you:

> 1. **Identify ways to increase your savings**
> 2. **Fund your savings program**
> 3. **Accumulate funds to begin your investment program**

It doesn't take a lot of money to start investing. Unit 8, Investing With Small Dollar Amounts, provides examples of investments that require as little as $25 for a U.S. savings bond or $250, $500, or $1,000 to open a mutual fund account, depending on account requirements.

Strategies for Saving Money to Invest

Establish a Regular Savings Program

The first strategy is to set up a regular savings program if you do not already have one. Saving means putting money aside from present earnings to provide for a known or unexpected need in the future. It is an integral part of family and personal financial planning. Having a specific goal provides motivation to save. You probably will not get very far saving for the sake of saving.

Needs versus Wants

Individuals and families save to satisfy their needs and wants. **Needs** are items that are necessary for survival such as food, shelter, clothing, and medical care. **Wants** are all the other things we think we need, but could do without. If we spend our money to satisfy wants before we meet our needs, we will probably experience financial difficulties. The pressure to acquire present wants is often greater than the willingness to provide for future needs or even future wants.

Generally speaking, four major financial needs require planning for in the near and distant future:

> 1. **Emergencies** from the normal course of living such as car repairs or replacing a major appliance
> 2. **Loss of income** as a result of death, divorce, disability, or unemployment
> 3. **Other family goals** such as education for your children or a special vacation
> 4. **Retirement**

Once goals have been set, a major thought in most people's minds is "How am I going to reach this goal? There is no way I can save that much money!" However, most people find that, if they really put their minds to it and they have set realistic goals, they can save the necessary money.

Notes

As we noted earlier, a regular savings program is critical to a family's immediate well-being as well as their long-term security. To adequately fund a savings program and begin an investment program, you must identify a specific amount to save from each paycheck and honor that commitment. Regular savings in small amounts is generally more effective than setting aside larger sums at sporadic intervals. As your salary increases, increase the amount you commit to savings.

Pay Yourself First

Another important concept for your savings program is to "pay yourself first." Make your "savings bill" a part of your spending plan, just like rent or mortgage payments, utility bills, clothing, car payments and upkeep, child care, or any other bill that you normally incur. When you pay your other bills, pay your savings bill by depositing the money into a savings account or other financial instrument. One painless way to accomplish this is payroll deduction if it is available. Your employer deposits your savings directly from your paycheck into a credit union, bank account, or a money market fund for a higher interest rate. If you never see the money, you won't miss it or be tempted to use it for something else before it reaches your savings account. Note how quickly small amounts of money can grow with time (table 1).

Table 1. How $10.00 a Month Will Grow

	Interest Rate												
Years	3%	4%	5%	6%	7%	8%	9%	10%	11%	12%	13%	14%	15%
1	$122	$122	$123	$124	$125	$125	$126	$127	$127	$128	$129	$130	$130
2	247	249	253	256	258	261	264	267	270	272	275	278	281
3	376	382	389	359	402	408	415	421	428	435	442	449	457
4	509	520	532	544	555	567	580	592	605	618	632	646	660
5	646	665	683	701	720	740	760	781	802	825	848	872	897
6	788	812	841	868	897	926	957	989	1,023	1,058	1,094	1,132	1,171
7	933	968	1,008	1,046	1,086	1,129	1,173	1,220	1,268	1,320	1,374	1,430	1,490
8	1,083	1,129	1,182	1,234	1,289	1,348	1,409	1,474	1,543	1,615	1,692	1,773	1,859
9	1,238	1,297	1,366	1,435	1,507	1,585	1,667	1,755	1,849	1,948	2,054	2,168	2,288
10	1,397	1,472	1,559	1,647	1,741	1,842	1,850	2,066	2,190	2,323	2,467	2,621	2,787
15	2,270	2,461	2,684	2,923	3,188	3,483	3,812	4,279	4,589	5,046	5,557	6,129	6,769
20	3,283	3,668	4,128	4,644	5,240	5,929	6,729	7,657	8,736	9,991	11,455	13,163	15,160
25	4,460	5,141	5,980	6,965	8,148	9,574	11,295	13,379	15,906	18,976	22,714	27,273	32,841
30	5,827	6,940	8,357	10,095	12,271	15,003	18,445	22,793	28,302	35,299	44,206	55,571	70,098

The table can be used to find out how long it will take to reach your financial goals. It shows the growth of monthly $10 deposits invested at various interest rates. Put aside $10 a month for five years at 10%, for example, and you'll have $781—the figure at the intersection of the year five and 10% interest columns. If you can invest $50 each month, you will have five times $781, or $3,905.

* *Adapted from* How To Save $1,000 Or More A Year. *Denise M. Matejic, Rutgers Cooperative Extension Service. Other Sources: Garman, E. T. and Forgue, R. E. (1991). Personal finance. Houghton Mifflin Company; Kiplinger's Retirement Report (1994, February).*

Save Bonus Money

Saving "bonus" money is also an easy strategy. Bonus money is money earned or received that was not expected, such as tax refunds, gift money, overtime pay,

rebates, and refunds. Saving this money over time will boost your saving dollars and provide a larger balance on which to earn interest for the future. (Note: If you consistently receive a large tax refund, you may want to adjust your withholding. A tax refund means that the government has had your money interest-free during the year; you were losing the use of the money to fund your financial goals.)

Save Coupon Money

Another strategy to boost your savings is to save coupon money. Many people use coupons to reduce their grocery and personal care bills, but few think of actually saving the money they saved! To make this strategy a reality, put aside the amount you "saved" by using coupons at the grocery store or drugstore. The amount saved is probably printed on each receipt. Put the "savings" (the money you did not spend) in a special "coupon saving jar." Every month or so add this cash to your savings account. Saving just $2 a week for 52 weeks gives you a savings total of $104 which could be your "seed" money to open an investment account. However, remember that you aren't saving if you buy something that you don't need or that costs more than a comparable product even with the coupon.

Continue Installment Loan Repayments

Most of us have one or more installment loans that we are repaying. Once you pay off an installment loan (assuming other loans are not overdue), continue to make "payments" to your savings account. For example, when you pay off your car loan, continue writing a check for the same amount, but make the check payable to your savings account. You were able to get along without this money for the duration of the car loan, so continue to live at the same level and save the "car payment." This is a good way to save for the down payment on your next car when the old car needs to be replaced. It also adds a substantial amount of money to your savings account on a regular basis. This same strategy can be used when other household expenses end (e.g., childcare).

Collect Loose Change

Another painless strategy is to collect loose change. At the end of each day, empty out your pockets and wallet and put the change in a special container. Every other week or once a month, deposit the change in your savings account. Don't cheat on yourself by "stealing" change that has been collected. Take it all to the bank. Some people even go so far as to keep all their change. They only pay for cash purchases with bills and save all their coins. Develop a plan that works for you and stick to it.

Save Lunch Money

Saving lunch money is another way you and your family can save money. Get up ten minutes earlier and make your own lunch. Save the money you would have spent on lunch. If all family members do this, the family can realize a nice sum that they can add to their savings. Working together to reach a family goal, such as a new TV or a summer vacation, can be an excellent family activity.

Shop for Sale Prices

Another strategy that can work for all family members on a wide variety of purchases is to save the money you "save" when you buy items on sale. When you buy an item on sale, save the difference between the sale price you paid and the "full" price you would have paid if the item had not been on sale. Put this money in a safe place and on a regular basis deposit it into your savings or investment account. Using this strategy can add large amounts to your savings program. The key is that you actually save this difference and apply it to your savings or investment program.

Plan a "Nothing Week"

Once in a while, have a "Nothing Week," an entire week when you and your family agree not to spend any more money than is absolutely necessary. You would not go to the movies, out to eat, bowling, etc. Plan to do special activities, but save the money instead of spending it. Add this money to your savings program. Another similar strategy is to use a crash budget approach. A crash budget works like a crash diet—you try to cut out all unnecessary spending and save as much as possible in a given period of time, say two weeks or a month. Add all the savings to your savings or investment program. If the "Crash Budget" sounds unbearable, consider a "Cut-Back Week." During this week, do what the family would normally do, but think of ways to make it less expensive and save the difference. For example, rent a movie instead of going to the theater, make long-distance phone calls on the weekend when the rates are lower, write a letter or send an e-mail instead of calling, drink mix-your-own lemonade instead of soft drinks, etc.

Avoid Paying Credit Charges

A critical savings strategy to consider is avoiding the use of credit. Unless credit purchases are paid off in full each month, interest consumes dollars that could be spent funding your saving and investing goals. Suppose that you have a balance of $1,000 on a credit card that carries a 19.8% interest rate and a full grace period. If you make no more charges against the account and only pay the minimum payment of 3% per month, you will pay approximately $165 in interest over one year. If you continue making only minimum monthly payments for the rest of the $1,000 with no additional charges, you will take eight years and three months to pay it off, and you will have paid $843 in interest.

Carefully evaluate all spending decisions, especially those being paid with credit. Make every spending decision on the basis of how it will satisfy your goals. Eliminate spending for items that have little or no value relative to your goals. Also be aware of your needs and wants as you make purchases.

Breaking Habits Can Yield Dollars to Invest

Some of the items we buy are needs, items that are necessary for survival. Other purchases are wants, all the things we think we need but could do without. Buying items to satisfy our wants can become a habit; before we know it, we are spending lots of money on these items. Find money to improve your financial situation by identifying some of your money habits. Then break those habits or at least reduce the number of times you enjoy the habit each day, week, or month. Review table 2 for specific examples.

Table 2. Looking For Money

Cable TV		$40/month=	$480/year
Video rentals	3@ $9/weekend =	$36/month=	$432/year
Movie tickets	2@ $7/visit =	$14/month=	$168/year
Treats at movie	2@ $5/visit =	$10/month=	$120/year
Dry cleaning	$4.50/garment @ 3 garments/month =		$162/year
Car wash	$5/week =	$20/month=	$240/year

Going further, if your family drinks iced tea instead of a 2-liter soda for the evening meal, you can probably save at least $5 a week or $260 ($5 x 52 = $260) a year. By drinking tap water instead of other beverages, you can save $7 a week or $364 ($7 x 52 = $364) a year. Let's look at those who feed the soda machines at work. By bringing soda from home ($.30 each) instead of feeding the machine ($.75 each), a person who drinks two sodas per day could save $234 over the course of a year ($.75-$.30 = $.45; $.45 x 2/day = $.90/day; $.90/day x 5 days/week = $4.50/week; $4.50/week x 52 weeks = $234/year). Changing or adjusting a few habits can result in big savings for you and your family. To see how easy this can be, use the following steps to help you identify and change habits.

Steps to Breaking Money Habits

Step 1.	Identify the habit, determine frequency, and calculate total cost
Step 2.	Make a decision to change
Step 3.	Act immediately
Step 4.	Share your plan
Step 5.	Stick with your plan to change
Step 6.	Celebrate your success

By following these six easy steps, you can gain better control of your financial resources and increase the money available for investing. Put this six-step plan to work for you and your family.

Step 1. Identify the habit, determine frequency, and calculate total cost

Using the worksheet, "So Where's The Money?," think of some habits you might be able to adjust. Select from the products or services listed or add your own choices to the list. Then determine how often you purchase the product or service. Next, calculate the total cost of enjoying the product or service for one year. Armed with this information, you are ready to advance to Step 2 in your quest to break habits and collect funds for investing.

Worksheet: So Where's the Money?

How often do you use the following?		
Product or Service	How Often Used	Monthly Cost x 12=Yearly Cost
Example: Hair Care	4 times/month	$100.00 x 12=$1200.00
Hair/Nail Care		
Dry Cleaning		
Eating Out		
Cell Phones/Pagers		
Vending machines/snacks		
Music CDs/Tapes		
Cigarettes/Alcohol		
Brand Name Clothes/Shoes		
Video Rentals		
Cable Television		
Movie Tickets/Snacks		
Pay-Per-View Television		
Bingo/Video Poker/Lottery		
Video Purchases		

Note: This discussion assumes a four-week month, which amounts to a 48-week year rather than a 52-week year. Therefore, savings will be understated.

Calculate your total monthly and yearly costs. Are you happy with where your money is going? If you aren't, now is the time to learn about ways to break habits and begin a savings program for you and your family.

Step 2. Make a decision to change

The second step to breaking habits involves looking for alternatives and choosing a different way of spending your money. This action step demands that you take control of the situation. One way to do this is to review your money habits and where you spend money, then identify how you can make changes. For example, have you ever stopped to consider how much you and other family members are spending for hair and nail care? If you spend $15.00 per week each month for hair care, that's $60.00 per month or $720.00 per year. Add a nail care bill of $15.00 per month or $180.00 per year. That is a lot of money.

What can you do? It is important for you and other family members to look good and feel good about yourselves. You can take control and make changes that will

help you capture some of the money going to these expenditures and redirect its use toward other family goals and still be well-groomed. "How can I do that?" you ask. Learn how to do these tasks yourself, or barter with a friend or neighbor who has these skills. You do something for them that they can't do, and they do your hair and nails. Every once in a while, you might treat yourself or other family members to a special makeover. Otherwise, save the money you would be spending on hair and nail care, and put this money toward your family goals.

Once you get into the swing of breaking habits, you and your family can come up with ideas on how to change and adjust spending.

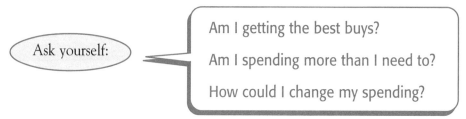

Ask yourself:

Am I getting the best buys?

Am I spending more than I need to?

How could I change my spending?

Be specific and honest as you review expenditures. Come up with creative ways to save money, and share these ideas with others. Here is an example from the clothing area to get you started.

✓ First, do inventories of each person's clothing: evaluate items—which are still usable, need replacing, or need to be added?

✓ Once you know what needs to be purchased, check out sales at different stores and look for the best buys.

✓ Avoid buying designer clothing, as it is usually very expensive. Ask yourself and family members if it is worth the extra cost.

✓ Consider what else you could buy if you bought items that cost less and had money left.

✓ Check out secondhand outlets, flea markets, thrift stores, and manufacturers' outlet stores.

✓ Be a knowledgeable shopper; don't think that the outlet stores are always cheaper than other stores.

✓ Know the prices of what you plan to buy and comparison shop for the best deal. Make simple repairs.

✓ Swap clothing with family and friends.

✓ Develop a positive attitude about recycled clothing and share that attitude with your children.

✓ Well-maintained clothing from relatives and friends can greatly enhance a wardrobe.

✓ When shopping for clothes, read all care labels very carefully.

✓ Only buy washable items.

✓ Dry cleaning can become quite expensive over the life of a garment.

By adopting these strategies, you will see your clothing budget shrink. Add the money you no longer spend on clothing to your investment plan. With these budget reduction ideas for clothing in mind, brainstorm ways to save money in other budget categories with family, friends, neighbors, and coworkers. Develop money-saving lists for:

$$$

- ✓ Using utilities
- ✓ Buying home furnishings
- ✓ Purchasing health and beauty aids
- ✓ Shopping in the grocery store
- ✓ Buying a car (new and/or used)
- ✓ Selecting telephone and cable television features
- ✓ Buying toys and other gift items
- ✓ Selecting insurance coverage
- ✓ Financing large ticket items and other purchases

$$$

For more information on saving money, access a copy of *66 Ways to Save Money* from the Internet at <www.ftc.gov/bcp/conline/pubs/general/66ways/index.html>. Some habits are very hard to break even when they are dangerous to our health and physical well-being as well as financial well-being. Examples that quickly come to mind are smoking, overeating, drinking alcohol, and gambling. These activities can be life-threatening and/or result in financial ruin. If you smoke a pack of cigarettes a day, what is the cost for a year? A pack-a-day habit adds up fast:

$4/pack/day = $28/week = a whopping $1,456/year

Remember, if you believe in yourself, you can kick any habit. Once you get into the swing of breaking habits, you and your family can come up with numerous ideas on how to change and adjust spending. Perhaps together the family could turn the task of saving into a friendly competition for the "Saver of the Year Award." The winner would be the person who saved the most dollars or the largest percentage of their income in a given period of time. By making the decision to change, you are ready to advance to Step 3 in breaking habits and finding money to invest.

Step 3. Act immediately

Now that you have all these great ideas to keep more of your money, how will you keep yourself motivated? Writing down your new desired behavior is one strategy. By recording the change, you are committing yourself to a new behavior. It is necessary to start your new behavior immediately. For best results, begin within 24 hours after making the decision to change or adjust spending. The sooner you begin a new behavior, the sooner the new behavior will become a habit. Step 4 will further assist you in adopting new behaviors.

Step 4. Share your plan

To further establish a new behavior, share your plan with others. Tell family, friends, and coworkers about your plan. By giving others the opportunity to support you, you boost your determination to succeed. If your behavior change involves the entire family, all family members must work together for the family to succeed. Refer back to the worksheet, "So Where's The Money?" Go over the chart with the entire family. Together, decide ways the family can break habits and develop a savings plan. Now is also a good time to make a family "piggy bank." The "bank" can be an empty jar or a small box. Once the family decides on their family financial goal, they can put a picture identifying the goal on the "bank."

Examples of goals include paying off a bill, buying something for the house, visiting family in another state, or accumulating money for school shoes. The "bank" needs to be kept where all can see it, and all can help by adding money. After accumulating a sum of money, the family might want to open a savings account at a local bank or credit union. Once this account has grown to cover emergencies, additional savings may then be invested so the family will realize a larger return on their money. Even with the best of intentions, sometimes staying focused on your savings plan is hard. The next step of the action plan will help you move forward.

Step 5. Stick with your plan to change

Step 5 is a critical step toward breaking habits and increasing family savings. You and family members must always look for new ways to reduce spending and increase savings. It is important to reinforce the fact that you can change your attitudes and break habits. Stay focused on your goal. It takes about 30 days for a new behavior to become a habit. Here are some specific activities for you and your family that will help you gain control of your finances but still have fun as a family. By engaging in activities such as these, we are changing our attitudes and choosing activities that are more "money friendly." Changing attitudes and lifelong habits will serve you well immediately and over a lifetime and set an example for your children by instilling the value of saving.

✓ **Plan a family outing.** Choose activities that are free or inexpensive, such as attending a free concert in the park, visiting a museum, borrowing videos from the library, or attending story hour at the library.

✓ **Plan a family night.** Have a special treat, ask family members to share a talent, remind family members how much you appreciate everyone working together to cut back spending. Together, count the money that the family has saved, talk about the goal toward which the family is saving, and how soon you think you will reach the goal.

✓ **Have a "make your own pizza" night.** Instead of going out for pizza, put the difference of the cost of food prepared at home and the cost of eating out in the family "bank."

✓ **Pack lunches instead of eating out.**

> ✓ Look for food specials at fast food restaurants. Bring home the food as a surprise instead of taking the kids out. Not only is this a money saver but a time saver and stress reducer (no arguments over where to go and what to eat).
>
> ✓ Video rental might be less costly than going to the movies. Swapping weeks to rent videos with neighbors might be less costly than going each weekend yourself. Borrow videos from the public library.

Yes, you can do it—you can change your attitude. You can break habits and save for things that are really important to you and your family. You just have to stick with your plan. If you are successful, you will reach Step 6 of our action plan.

Step 6. Celebrate your success

The last step to breaking habits is to celebrate your success. Once you have reached your initial goals, let others know of your success. Enjoy the fruits of your savings. Then continue with your new behaviors that are now habits. You have the tools necessary to be successful. Remember to trim all unnecessary expenses and keep your needs and wants in perspective. Watch the pennies you save grow into dollars that can be used to fund your saving and investment programs.

Be a Comparison Shopper

Comparison shopping is the customer's best, but least used, technique when spending regardless of the type of expenditure. Comparing prices and products can save as much as 50% off a price you might have paid without making the comparison. Comparison shopping makes good sense. It is important to remember that an overspender isn't just someone who spends more than he earns but also anyone who pays too much for things, especially when items or services purchased are conveniently available for less. Internet shoppers can find comparison shopping resources at <www.mysimon.com> and <www.bestwebbuys.com>. The benefits of comparison shopping are more than the money saved. Comparison shopping puts you in control of your finances. It helps you learn more about the products and services you are interested in buying. As a more informed consumer, you are able to make better spending decisions. Additionally, each success will reinforce your resolve to comparison shop again. By making wise consumer decisions and getting a good value for less, shoppers are able to save and/or invest the money saved.

Untapped Strategies: Potential Money Sources to Fund Your Investment Program

Do you know that sometimes you can collect dollars instead of pennies by becoming a more knowledgeable consumer? By using the strategies that follow, you may be able to add large sums of money to your family's savings and investment program. Throughout the country, billions of dollars remain in accounts that have

been abandoned or forgotten. These accounts include checking and saving accounts, pension benefits, and insurance benefits. How could anyone possibly forget about something of value? Well, maybe.... You neglected to retrieve a security deposit after moving out of an apartment. Perhaps dividends on a stock or mutual fund have been going to the wrong address. Maybe you switched banks and failed to close out all your old accounts. Or you changed jobs frequently and previous employers don't know where to send pension benefits. Perhaps you are entitled to benefits of a life insurance policy or cash left by a relative who has died. In any event, you might be entitled to unclaimed property held by your state or the Pension Benefit Guaranty Corporation. Or you might be the beneficiary of a long-lost insurance policy. Fortunately, receiving your just rewards is not extremely difficult if you know how to proceed.

To locate missing bank accounts and other unclaimed cash, contact your state's unclaimed property office or visit the Web site <www.missingmoney.com>. In most states, owners can recover their cash whenever they learn about it, no matter how long it has been in the state fund. About half of the states pay interest on money left in interest-bearing accounts. Instead of waiting for a state to find you, which is unlikely, you can contact the state's unclaimed property office. If you have access to the Internet, the CapitaLink site on the World Wide Web (<www.ifast.com>) allows you to search $50 million in unclaimed mutual fund, insurance, and financial accounts at no charge. It also lists all of the states' unclaimed property offices.

When you write or call about abandoned property, give your name (maiden or former names, if necessary), Social Security number, current address, and all previous addresses while you lived in the state. If you are applying for property that was held in someone else's name, provide his or her Social Security number and former addresses. States normally take two to three weeks to write back saying whether there is property waiting for you. If you are due a windfall, they will send you an abandoned-property claim form to complete.

Return the completed form with proof that the cash belongs to you. If it's in your name, you will need to supply only a current ID, such as a copy of your driver's license, and any document that links you to the money (e.g., a pay stub, savings passbook, or utility bill). For property that belonged to you when you lived at an earlier address, you must provide proof that you lived there. A copy of a tax return will do. Expect to get your check in about two months.

From time to time, you may see advertisements of asset finders, people who offer to find lost property for you. Beware of such ads. If you decide to hire such a firm, pay no more than 10% of the assets recovered and check out the firm with the Better Business Bureau. According to one state property fund director, "If you ever get a card or letter from a company offering to find your money, take that as a tip that the firm knows you have money waiting. So call or write to the state fund yourself. Then you'll get all the money you're due."

According to the Pension Benefit Guaranty Corporation (PBGC), more than 7,000 people in the United States are owed uncollected pension benefits. The PBGC, a

federal agency, has launched a nationwide search on the Internet to find workers who are owed benefits and who could not be located when pension plans closed. To check if your name is on the list of hard-to-find beneficiaries, log on to the Pension Search Directory at <www.pbgc.gov/search>. The directory identifies about 1,000 companies mainly in the transportation, machinery, retail trade, apparel, and financial services industries. If you do not have a computer, check for availability at a public library or libraries at high schools, community colleges, or universities. If you are not able to access a computer and you feel you are owed benefits, write to the Pension Benefit Guaranty Corporation, Missing Participant Program, 1200 K Street, NW, Suite 930, Washington, DC 20005. Include the participant's or beneficiary's name, address, daytime telephone number, Social Security number, date of birth, and the name and location of the employer.

Another place to look for lost cash is the Internal Revenue Service. Yes, the IRS has more than $68 million in unclaimed tax-refund checks that were returned because of an incorrect address or other delivery problems. The average check amount is $690. If you think you are owed a tax refund, but have not received it, call the IRS at 1-800-829-1040.

The last place where you might look for ready cash is lost insurance policies, yours or those of relatives where you might be the beneficiary. If you think there is a lost policy in your family, send a stamped, self-addressed business envelope to the Missing Policy Service, American Council of Life Insurance, 1001 Pennsylvania Avenue, NW, Washington, DC 20004-2599. The Council will send you a tracer form to complete and return. The Council will then circulate copies to about 100 large life insurance companies. The service is free and takes from three to six months.

Strategies to Stretch Your Money

Whether you save pennies to make dollars, break habits and bank the savings, or find that you are the beneficiary of a long-lost life insurance policy, you are the one who has to manage your funds to best meet your individual and/or family goals. Remember that saving money does not make one a tightwad. On the contrary, saving money often allows you to have more of what is important to you and your family. As you continue on your path to saving money, you may find that the following ideas will serve you well as road marks on your journey.

Adopt the Two-Week Rule

If you think you really want something, wait two weeks to get it. The purpose of this habit is to make you an impulse saver, not an impulse spender. The two-week rule does not mean losing out on a once-in-a-lifetime opportunity. How many items, such as expensive clothing, a new piece of furniture, a boat or recreational vehicle, or a new car, would not be there in two weeks? If you wait two weeks to buy big-ticket items, two good things can happen. You may find the same item less expensive somewhere else. Or you may discover that you really did not want the item once the initial excitement wore off.

Notes

Avoid Unnecessary Waste

Another principle to practice is keeping items that are still good. You can avoid waste, which translates into savings or more money for other activities. You don't have to keep using items that need to be replaced, but do continue using those that still have value. The money that you would use for premature replacements can fund your savings and investment programs or purchase other goods and services for you and your family.

In a similar vein, don't waste goods and services. Don't leave the television on when nobody is watching it or operate the air conditioner when nobody is going to be in the house for hours. Don't throw away a tube of toothpaste that is good for a few more brushes. These actions are related to the conservation of resources, not money; but in the end you save money, too. Another related principle is to develop a positive philosophy regarding care and maintenance of goods. By taking proper care of products, using them in the intended manner, and maintaining them according to manufacturer's instructions, you can greatly extend the useful life of an item. Instead of buying a new item, use the well-cared-for item and invest the money you would have spent. Let it be earning interest for you and contributing to your long-term financial security.

Become a Coupon Clipper

Would you think it was crazy to take a few dollar bills out of your wallet each week and throw them into the garbage can? That is exactly what you are doing by not using coupons for items that you normally buy or taking advantage of dozens of money-saving opportunities each day. If you spent five minutes a week cutting out coupons for your grocery shopping and saved at least $6.00 a week, that is the same as getting paid $72.00 an hour after taxes. In a year, you would save a minimum of $300.00. You would need to deposit $5,000.00 and get a 6% yield tax-free to make that much money. Remember, pennies do make dollars.

And finally, practice treating yourself. Having saved money by not buying things you don't need allows you to spend money for the things you want and that make your life enjoyable. Learn to truly enjoy the fruits of your labor.

Summary

If you are able to provide the desire and self-discipline, you will be able to "find" the money necessary to fund your saving and investment programs. Improving your financial health through increased savings is not a matter of luck, rather it reflects planning, defined goals, wise decisions, and a desire for personal success. The various savings strategies included in this unit offer you the groundwork needed to initiate a saving and investment program for you and your family. To help you stay on target, see "21 Ways to Keep More Cash" for reinforcement and additional strategies.

21 Ways to Keep More Cash

Notes

1. Pay yourself first. Have automatic contributions from your paycheck or checking account go to a savings or investment plan. Money that you do not see is often easier to save.

2. Find money to save by refinancing your mortgage. Cutting your rate by a percentage point will probably pay off if you plan to be in your home for an additional 18 months. (Note: This depends on the closing costs required.)

3. Switch to a credit card that charges a lower interest rate, but be aware of low rates that increase after 6–12 months. Be ready to switch cards again.

4. If you are offered a no-fee, no-points home equity loan, sign up. Use this line of credit to pay off higher-cost debt. Do not use it to increase your debt load.

5. Pay ahead on your mortgage. An extra $25–$50 a month can make a big difference in the amount of interest you pay as well as the number of years you pay. Or pay your monthly payment in two installments (if allowed)— one payment two weeks before the due date and the other on the due date. You will reduce the total cost of the mortgage and the length of the loan.

6. If you are incurring late fees or extra finance charges because bills come due before you get paid, ask to have the due date changed to after payday.

7. If you have a computer, cut your telephone costs by e-mailing children in college and far-off friends. Other money-saving tips include buying your own phone and blocking "900" numbers if you have youngsters.

8. To cut your utility bill, unplug the extra refrigerator or freezer that is used infrequently. Also lower the thermostat on your water heater to 120 degrees, install high-efficiency showerheads and faucets, switch to compact fluorescent bulbs in fixtures that are on at least four hours a day, replace an inefficient heating and cooling system if you are likely to stay in your current house for a decade or more, and check with your utility company to see if they have programs that will pay you to insulate your home.

9. Sign up for overdraft protection on your checking account; dodge unnecessary bank fees; avoid keeping large balances in your checking or savings accounts earning low interest rates—invest them in higher-yielding investments; and compare costs of checks from your bank and other sources for the best buy. Join a credit union for potential savings on your banking and credit transactions.

10. Shop for the best price on all your insurance needs. Reduce costs by having home and auto insurance with one insurer, installing safety devices in your home, canceling private mortgage insurance (PMI) when you have sufficient equity in your home, purchasing life insurance only on breadwinner(s) or primary care-givers, and avoiding single-disease health insurance policies.

11. If available, use your employer's plan that lets you set aside part of your salary to pay medical bills with pretax dollars. Carefully evaluate health care plans available to you and select the one that best meets your needs.

12. Comparison shop for the best prices on prescription drugs; when available, use generic drugs for both prescription and over-the-counter drugs, and utilize mail-order pharmacies for drugs taken regularly. ▶

13. If you smoke, stop. It is bad for your health and costs about $700 a year for a pack-a-day smoker. A year after you quit, check with your life insurance agent for reduced premiums.

14. Save big by buying a nearly new rather than a brand-new car. Other savings related to your car include pumping your own gas, buying the octane fuel recommended for your car, raising your collision and comprehensive deductibles to $500, and avoiding four-wheel drive vehicles unless needed (they cost more up front and you pay more for gas, tires, and insurance). If you buy a new car, order from the factory, selecting only the options you want unless the dealer is willing to discount the price of unwanted options.

15. Buy in bulk at discount and warehouse stores. Always shop with a list to avoid impulse buys and use coupons when appropriate. Try store brands for considerable savings.

16. Instead of beginning your landscaping projects the first warm day of spring when plants and related materials are most expensive, wait until the items go on sale.

17. Encourage your college-bound students to apply for scholarships and offer to pay them a lump sum to graduate on time to avoid having to pay a fifth year of college. If your child attends college at least 150 miles away, check with your agent regarding lowering your auto insurance premium (it could drop as much as one-third). Even if the student takes the car to school, costs may be lower due to the location of the school.

18. Maximize contributions to your tax-deferred retirement plan and contribute to an IRA. Even though you may not be able to deduct IRA contributions from your income, the money in your account grows tax-deferred until it is taken out.

19. To save dollars on your entertainment and education budget categories, use the local library. They have the latest books, magazines, journals, and newspapers as well as music compact discs, Internet access, investment research, and a host of other services.

20. Other quick ways to add cash back into your budget include canceling subscriptions to magazines you do not read or could access at the library, dropping club memberships you do not use, canceling credit cards you no longer use, disconnecting cable television or at least dropping some of the options you probably have, and trimming back the options you carry on the telephone.

21. Catch your coins and bank your surprises. At the end of each day, put all your loose change into a savings container and once a month deposit the collection into your savings account. Whenever you receive a raise or unexpected money such as a gift or contest winnings, put all or part of the money into your savings account.

Compiled by Joyce H. Christenbury, Clemson University Cooperative Extension Service, May 1996.

Action Steps

✔ Take action now.
Finding Money to Invest

Check off the steps after you have completed them.

- ❏ Establish an emergency fund containing an amount equal to three to six months of your income.

- ❏ Determine amount of money needed to fund your high-cost goals (house, education, retirement, etc.).

- ❏ Develop a plan to ensure that you save the money needed to fund your goals.

- ❏ Set up a regular savings program, if you do not already have one.

- ❏ Identify two strategies you could implement to help you accumulate funds to invest.

- ❏ Identify a money-consuming habit you have that you would be willing to change.

- ❏ Calculate the amount of money you can realize in one year by changing this habit.

- ❏ Change your behavior, save the appropriate amount of money, and invest it.

- ❏ Track your investment and watch it grow.

References

Consumer Literacy Consortium. (1998, April). *66 ways to save money.* Consumer Federation of America.

Chatzky, J. S. (1998, May 29–31). Save your change—it could grow to thousands of dollars. *USA Weekend,* 11.

Cruz, H. (1996, April 15). Saving money does not make one a tightwad. *The Greenville News,* D1.

Detweiler, Gerri. (1993). *The ultimate credit handbook.* New York: Penguin Group.

Folsom, David. (1997, September 15). Finding money made easy. *Bottom Line Personal,* 8.

Kiplinger Washington Editors, Inc. (1998, September). $13 million in missing pensions. *Kiplinger's Retirement Report 5 (9),* 6.

NCFE. (1997). Do without a little now...gain a lot more later on. *The NCFE Motivator Newsletter,* 3.

O'Neill, B. (1997). Public policy: Creating an environment for increased U.S. savings, U.S. savings rates: An overview. *AAFCS Family Economics and Resource Management Biennial,* 1–4.

Personal income and outlays. (1999, March). Washington, DC: U.S. Department of Commerce, Bureau of Economic Analysis Web site <www.bea.doc.gov/bea/dn/pitbl.htm>.

Razzi, E. (1998, September). 33 ways to save at home. *Kiplinger's Personal Finance Magazine,* 111–116.

Sheets, K. & Spears, G. (1996, May). 101 ways to keep more cash. *Kiplinger's Personal Finance Magazine,* 32–39.

Author Profile

Joyce H. Christenbury, M.Ed., CFCS, is Professor Emerita of Family and Youth Development with the Clemson University Cooperative Extension Service. As an extension family resource management specialist, she provided leadership in the area of family resource management with an emphasis on helping individuals and families develop skills needed to cope with today's complex marketplace. Professor Christenbury received her undergraduate degree in Home Economics Education from Winthrop University, Rock Hill, South Carolina, and her masters from the University of North Carolina at Greensboro in housing, management, and equipment. Prior to joining the Clemson faculty in 1973, Christenbury taught in the College of Home Economics at the University of Delaware in Newark, Delaware.

Ownership INVESTING

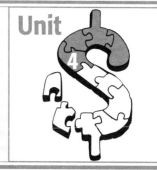

Irene Leech, Ph.D., CFCS, Virginia Polytechnic Institute and State University

Now that you know some basics about investing and ways to find money to invest, it's time to learn about the types of investments that are available. There are two basic categories of investments: ownership and loanership. **Equity** or **ownership** investing means becoming a partial owner of a company or piece of property through the purchase of investments such as stock, growth mutual funds, and real estate. With ownership investments, you have influence on some decisions made about the investment. For example, if you own stock, you may vote for members of the board of directors that makes decisions about the company or make proposals concerning its operations. If you own an apartment which you rent, you make decisions such as repainting and setting the rent price. When the value of an investment goes up, you share that increase with other owners; when it goes down, you share the loss.

When there are earnings, you share them. There are no guarantees about what the price of the investment will be should you want to sell it in the future. The price may be higher than it was when you bought the investment, but it could be lower. Likewise, there are no guarantees that there will be earnings (such as dividends) or of how much they will be. Price and earnings may be affected by the management of a company or by outside factors such as political changes, weather, and the national or world economy.

On the other hand, when you have a **loanership** investment, you simply loan your money to someone (e.g., a bank) and get an agreed upon return. Generally, when you invest larger sums of money and invest for longer periods of time, you earn more. If you want to learn more about these investments refer to Unit 5, "Fixed-Income Investing," in this home study series.

The focus of this unit is ownership investments. These investments, equities, can either be owned outright or purchased on credit. Examples of equities include stock, growth mutual fund shares, real estate, collectibles, commodities, and businesses. This unit will provide you with an overview of investment products available for purchase. If you are interested in investing in any of these products, you should learn more about their characteristics, as well as about the particular company or product, before investing.

EQUITY INVESTING
Becoming a partial owner of a company or piece of property through the purchase of investments such as stock, equity mutual funds, and real estate.

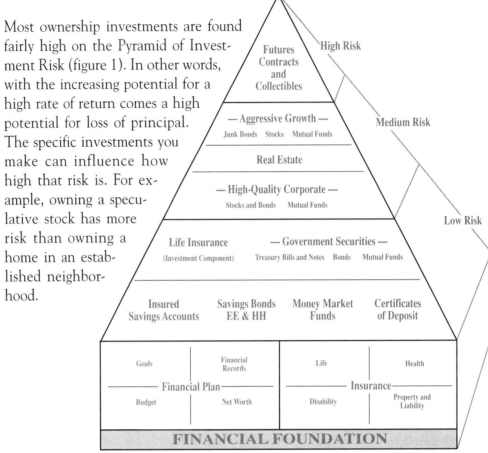

Most ownership investments are found fairly high on the Pyramid of Investment Risk (figure 1). In other words, with the increasing potential for a high rate of return comes a high potential for loss of principal. The specific investments you make can influence how high that risk is. For example, owning a speculative stock has more risk than owning a home in an established neighborhood.

Figure 1. Pyramid of Investment Risk.
Source: National Institute for Consumer Education, 1998

Common Stock

When a company wants to raise money, it offers investors a share of ownership in the company in the form of stock in exchange for that money. As a partial owner of the company, each investor shares in the success or failure of the business. There is no guarantee of return for the investment. Investors become part owners of a business and have no guarantee that they will receive any income for the use of their money or that they will get back any or all of their money in the future.

Over time, however, common stocks outperform all other investments. According to the Chicago investment research firm Ibbotson Associates, the average annual return on U.S. large company stocks from 1926 through 2000 was 11% versus 12.4% for small company stocks, 5.3% for long-term government bonds, and 3.8% for U.S. Treasury bills.

If a company makes money in a given time period, its board of directors may decide to reward its owners by distributing dividends or may choose to reinvest the money in the company. If you own a stock that pays dividends, you may have the option of reinvesting them in more stock instead of receiving a cash dividend. The dividends are still taxable but **dividend reinvestment plans** (also known as DRIPs) are an easy way to increase your investment holdings.

As owners of the business, stockholders elect directors who select the people who manage the company on a day-to-day basis. Depending upon the business and the way in which it is set up to operate, stockholders may have the opportunity to influence other decisions as well. Typically, this happens at an annual business meeting and stockholders can cast proxy votes if they are unable to attend the meeting in person.

Many companies offer stock investments. If you are interested in purchasing stock, you should learn about the industry and the particular business in which you are considering investing. There are many ways to learn. Magazines such as *Kiplinger's* and *Money* are one. Newspapers, especially those that focus on economic topics, like *The Wall Street Journal*, and those in large cities, such as *The New York Times*, are good sources. Companies such as *Value Line* produce materials to specifically rate stocks, and these are typically carried in the reference section of larger libraries.

The Internet is full of Web sites that offer information. Scrutinize Web sites to recognize the source, and note whether written material is produced by a person or business that may gain profit from the information provided. One place to look for such Web sites is in the money section of the site at <www.consumerworld.org>. There is a link there to the American Association of Independent Investors at <www.aaii.org>. There is also a link to a stock market simulation in which individuals can participate to learn more about how the market works (<www.thinkquest.org/library/lib/site_search.html>, click on "EduStock").

By law, a company must provide a prospectus, which describes information such as its management and financial situation when it first issues stock. If you are interested in purchasing new stock in a company, you can request a prospectus. You may also find prospectuses online at the Securities and Exchange Commission Web site (<www.sec.gov>). Some annual reports are available online from the Public Registers Annual Report Service at <www.prars.com>.

**DRIPs
DIVIDEND
REINVESTMENT
PLANS**
Plans that allow investors to automatically reinvest any dividends their stock pays in more stock shares.

Notes

Generally stocks are classified by category:

1. **Growth stocks** are those of companies that are expected to increase in value. They may have high P/E (price to earnings) ratios. This means that the price of the stock is high compared to the forecasted earnings. A high ratio tends to indicate a more speculative situation. A low ratio tends to indicate a more conservative investment.

2. **Income stocks** are those of companies that expect to pay regular, relatively high (compared to other companies) dividends.

3. **Speculative stocks** are those of companies that have potential for the future. They generally do not pay much in dividends, and their prices may be relatively volatile.

---

4. **Value stocks** currently have relatively low prices compared to their historical earnings and the value of the company's assets.

5. **Blue chip stocks** are those of established companies with relatively stable
stock prices and relatively predictable earnings.

6. **Penny stocks** are sold for $5 per share or less. They may be initial offerings
with prices set intentionally low or stocks of companies that are experienc-
ing difficult financial times. In either case, these are speculative stocks, and
if you invest in them, you should be prepared to lose all of your money.

*It is important to consider your goals and your needs when you invest in
stocks and to select ones that are most likely to match your situation.*

Investors use indexes to assess the general activity of the stock market. The Dow
Jones Industrial Average is the most widely followed gauge of daily market activity. It
includes 30 stocks in well-established companies. Other indexes include the **Standard & Poor's 500** (which includes 400 industrial companies, 40 financial institutions, 40 public utilities, and 20 transportation firms), the **New York Stock Exchange Composite** (all stocks traded on the New York Stock Exchange), the **American Stock Exchange Composite** (stocks traded on the American Stock Exchange),
and the **NASDAQ Composite** (newer stocks traded over-the-counter in the quota-
tions system of the National Association of Securities Dealers). These indexes are
widely reported in newspapers, on television and radio, and via the Internet. Indexes
help show trends in market behavior.

Investors use **Beta** as a measure of a stock's price volatility—how much it changes.
The average Beta for all stocks is +1. However, the Beta for an individual stock can
be either positive or negative. The larger the Beta figure (e.g., +2 versus .50), the
more speculative—and thus risky—a stock.

A "must read" for all equity investors is a company's annual report. Along with
other investor resources, such as *Value Line* and professional advisors, annual reports provide important clues to company performance. To obtain a company's annual report, call its "shareholder relations" department or request a copy online via
the company Web site. The first part of a company annual report is the letter to
shareholders. Here, company management explains significant changes in company operations (e.g., new products, decreased earnings) and in the report's financial statements (balance sheet and income statement).

Like a personal net worth statement, the **balance sheet** in an annual report lists a
company's assets and liabilities (debts) at a particular point in time (usually the end of a
company's fiscal year). Assets are things owned by a company, such as product inven-
tory and accounts receivable (money owed by customers). Liabilities are company obligations to pay for goods and services or to repay borrowed funds (e.g., interest and
principal on company bonds). The name "balance sheet" reflects the fact that figures
must "balance." The value of a company's assets must equal the sum of its liabilities and
shareholder equity (the total value of all shareholders' investments in a company).

Various financial ratios can be used to determine the financial health of a company. A common one is the **current ratio**, which is current (less than a year) assets divided by current liabilities. A 2:1 ratio ($2 of assets for every $1 of debt) is considered adequate. Another helpful ratio is the **debt-to-equity ratio**. This is a company's total liabilities divided by shareholder equity and should be less than 1:1.

Income statements in an annual report describe a company's net income (or loss) per share. A common ratio used to analyze income statements is **earnings per share**: net income divided by the number of outstanding shares. Another is the **price/earnings (P/E) ratio**. This is calculated by dividing the share price by earnings per share (e.g., $24 per share and $2 earnings per share = P/E of 12).

Stocks can be bought and sold on one of the nine major exchanges. Newspapers typically report on the New York Stock Exchange and the American Stock Exchange. Newer or less frequently traded stocks are sold by telephone or computer hookup rather than at an exchange, a process called **over-the-counter**.

Current information about stock prices and sales is available in most newspapers. An example of a newspaper report of the New York Stock Exchange is shown in figure 2. As of April 2001, all stock prices are reported in decimals instead of fractions.

NYSE

52-week High	52-week Low	Abbr.	Sales (000s)	Last	Chg
96.13	48.38	AT&T	12728	85.56	−2.44
51.25	22.94	Compaq	21938	32.75	−1.63
8.50	3.44	Ethyl	66	4.69	−0.13
68.00	47.44	Litton	53	56.94	+0.07

Figure 2. Example of newspaper report of the New York Stock Exchange (NYSE).

Terms in figure 2 — *52-week High-Low*: These numbers tell the highest and lowest prices at which the stock has sold in the last year. Prices are in dollars and decimals (e.g., the highest price AT&T stock sold for in the last year was $96.13 and the lowest price was $48.38). *Abbreviation (Abbr.)*: Standard abbreviation of the stock's name. For example, AT&T. *Sales (000s)*: Number of shares traded yesterday (multiplied by 1,000). AT&T sold 12,728,000 shares the previous selling day. *Last*: Price at closing yesterday. For AT&T, it was $85.56 per share. *Chg*: The difference in the closing price yesterday and the day before. The price today was $2.44 lower than yesterday's.

If you are interested in purchasing stocks, the cost of purchasing and selling stocks may include brokerage fees. Compare fees for the best deal on costs.

Many investors use a specific strategy to invest in stocks. **Dollar-cost averaging** is the strategy of regularly investing the same amount (e.g., $50) at regular intervals (e.g., monthly)—regardless of the price of the stock. When investors use the **buy and hold** strategy, they purchase stocks and keep them for a number of years, not worrying about the changes in the market. Investors refer to times when prices are very low as a **bear market** and times when they are high as a **bull market**. The goal of successful equity investing is to buy when prices are low and sell when prices are high. You can learn more about strategies in Unit 1, "Investment Basics."

**REIT
(REAL ESTATE
INVESTMENT
TRUST)**
A way to invest in real
estate by buying shares
of a company that
manages real estate.

Real Estate

This very popular investment alternative includes land, the permanent structures on land, and accompanying rights and privileges, such as crops and mineral rights. There are many ways that you can own real estate, and it is a very popular investment. In fact, a home is generally the single largest asset that most people have. Among the other ways to invest in real estate is owning rental houses and land for potential housing or commercial development. You can also invest in real estate indirectly by purchasing units in a real estate limited partnership or shares in a **real estate investment trust (REIT)**. Since direct ownership of real estate is so common, we will begin by discussing it.

When you purchase real estate, the costs of purchase include real estate commissions (which may technically be paid by the seller, but do influence the total cost of the property), transfer and recording fees charged by the state and/or local government, attorney fees, title search fees, appraisal fees, surveying fees, and inspection fees (these may be optional). If you need a loan to pay for the property, there will be additional fees related to the loan itself. One Web site where you can get information about buying a home is <www.homepath.com>.

There are also ongoing costs related to owning real estate. These vary according the type of structure and the location. The property must be maintained and protected through the purchase of insurance. Maintenance costs may include cutting grass, raking leaves, snow removal, or painting. At some point, the roof or furnace may have to be replaced. Insurance is needed to protect the structure and your liability related to it. There may also be annual property taxes.

Home ownership is encouraged through our income tax system, which provides an income tax deduction for mortgage interest and property taxes and generous tax exemptions on the increase in value realized when most homes are sold. However, tax benefits of ownership should be part of the reason for buying, not the only reason.

Real estate is fairly high in the investment risk pyramid. It is not a liquid investment. Although it is sometimes possible to quickly turn real estate into cash, it can also take a long time to find the right buyer. Also, while one can take care of one's own property, it is not possible to ensure that the property next door will be taken care of at the same level. A public change, such as a power line or road, or some other change, may increase or decrease the value of your property.

You may receive regular or irregular income from real estate, including rent for structures or the land itself, income from sales of crops such as timber or from gravel or minerals in the land. Costs are associated with each form of income. You can also make money on the sale of real estate when you are able to sell it for more than you paid for it and the costs in selling it. Real estate agents often say that the key to success in real estate investing is "location, location, location." Where your investment is, and what is near it will greatly influence its value.

In addition to directly investing in real estate, you can purchase it indirectly through real estate limited partnerships, real estate investment trusts (REITs), and owning mortgages. These are investments you will want to thoroughly investigate before purchasing.

Investors in real estate limited partnerships buy shares for unit costs of $500 or $1,000. The partnership invests in land or commercial real estate such as shopping malls and apartment complexes. A prorated share of rental income is passed on to investors as taxable income. When a partnership is liquidated or sold, any profits are distributed as capital gains.

When you buy shares in a real estate investment trust (REIT), the company manages various real estate investments. It may own real estate (e.g., apartment complexes and offices) and make money by renting the property or by making loans to others who own and manage property. Like a mutual fund, REITs provide diversification and professional management. They are required to distribute almost all of their annual income as dividends to investors. If the REIT portfolio is not properly managed or there are changes in the market, the principal investment may lose value.

You can select from over 300 REITs for investors. REIT shares, typically costing up to $40 each, are purchased from brokers and trade like stock on major exchanges. Additional information about REITs can be obtained from brokerage firms or the National Association of Real Estate Investment Trusts Web site <www.nareit.com>.

Equity Unit Investment Trusts

Unit investment trusts (UITs) were first issued in the 1960s as a way to "package" and sell portfolios of professionally selected bonds, especially tax-exempt municipal bonds. The cost of a unit is generally $1,000. During the 1990s, the UIT concept was extended to stocks. Unlike mutual funds, which are professionally managed, equity UITs are a "buy-and-hold" investment. Securities in the portfolio are held for a predetermined time to generate dividends and capital gains for investors. At maturity, investors can take their cash and invest elsewhere or can "roll over" their balance into a new UIT. Like their bond counterparts, equity UITs are an unmanaged portfolio of stocks that usually remains unchanged throughout the life of the trust. Some equity UITs follow a specific investment strategy such as investing in the five or ten highest yielding stocks among the 30 stocks included in the Dow Jones Industrial Average. Another is UITs that invest in stocks listed on foreign stock exchanges. Like mutual funds, an increasing number of equity UITs also select stocks from a particular industry sector (e.g., technology) or companies located in a particular state or region of the country.

Like individual stocks, UIT dividends and capital gains are taxable, whether earnings are distributed in cash or reinvested in additional UIT units. If the value of a UIT portfolio increases, that capital gain is taxed. Most equity UITs have maturi-

ties of six years or less. Shares can be sold prior to the trust's maturity at a price determined by market conditions. Two advantages of equity UITs are not having to worry about changes in portfolio holdings or management and tax efficiency (low taxes because stocks in a UIT portfolio are rarely traded). A major disadvantage is their up-front cost. Equity UITs typically charge a front-end load (commission) of about 3% to 5% of the amount invested.

Equity Mutual Funds

Mutual funds are professionally managed portfolios of securities and are described in detail in Unit 6. Options available for equity investors include:

✦ Growth Funds ✦ funds that typically invest in the stock of well-established companies with an objective of capital appreciation.

✦ Aggressive Growth Funds ✦ funds that invest in new companies without a track record or funds that use risky trading actions.

✦ Equity-Income Funds ✦ funds that invest in the stock of companies that are known for their payment of above-average dividends.

✦ Focus Funds ✦ funds that invest in a small number (e.g., 20 or 30) of stocks instead of the 100+ securities typical of most funds.

✦ Global Funds ✦ funds that invest in stocks worldwide, including those issued by companies located within the United States.

✦ Gold Funds ✦ funds that invest in gold mining companies or related securities (e.g., precious metals).

✦ Index Funds ✦ funds that include stocks that comprise a benchmark market index such as the Standard & Poor's 500 or Wilshire 5000.

✦ International Funds ✦ funds that invest only in stocks issued outside of the United States.

✦ Momentum Funds ✦ funds that invest in companies that are "hot" at the moment but tend to be very volatile as share prices change.

✦ Regional Funds ✦ funds that concentrate on companies located in one part of the world (e.g., Europe, Asia).

Collectibles

There are many things that you can collect as an investment. People collect stamps, coins, art, cars, autographs—just about anything. To be financially successful with collectibles as an investment, a high level of knowledge is required. Some people collect as a hobby and enjoy spending their time this way.

To make money with this type of investment, you need a collection of items in top condition—which probably means that you cannot regularly use or touch the collectible. It is necessary to safely store collectibles in an environment that will protect the items. Keep documented evidence of the value of your collection, (e.g., an appraisal of antiques). Regular maintenance, insurance, and storage may be necessary. The specific needs and the type of collectible will determine costs.

Generally, there is no regular or periodic income from collectibles. When you sell an item, you see the gain in value. When you want to sell, it could take a while to find the buyer willing to pay what you think your collectible is worth. A professional appraiser or auction house may also be required to sell items to other investors. As you make investment decisions about collectibles, make sure that you are truly focusing on the value of the investment and that you are not unduly influenced by the psychological pleasure you receive from owning it.

Business

Ownership of a business is another investment option. There are many different kinds of businesses and many ways to be involved. You may own and operate a business, or you could own the business and hire someone else to operate it. You can start your own business or purchase a franchise of a larger business. While there is certainly opportunity for income from businesses, there are also many risks. Careful attention must be given to the financing, cash flow needs, and reserves. It is important to separate businesses from the family budget. You want to avoid putting your house at risk, for example, because your business has difficult financial times.

In many states, Cooperative Extension offers education on micro- and home-based businesses. The Small Business Administration also offers assistance. Other organizations in communities and in state government have valuable resources. If you are considering such an investment, search widely for information. The failure rate of small businesses is very high. Planning, especially development of a business plan, is critical.

Commodities

At the very top of the investment risk pyramid are commodities. These include products such as pork, grain, coffee, sugar, etc. Financial expert Andrew Tobias says that since 90% of the people who speculate in commodities lose (and 98% may be a more accurate figure), the key is how to be among the 10% (or 2%) who win. He simply compares investing in commodities to gambling. At the top of the investment risk pyramid, you have high potential for return, but also high risk. To invest there, you need to be able to afford to lose your entire investment.

Costs include brokerage fees. You also need considerable knowledge of the commodity in question and the markets in which it is created and sold as well as the changing situations of the buyers.

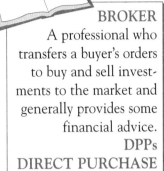

BROKER
A professional who transfers a buyer's orders to buy and sell investments to the market and generally provides some financial advice.
DPPs
DIRECT PURCHASE PLANS
"No load" stocks sold directly to investors without a broker.

Buying and Selling Equity Investments

There are many ways to purchase equity investments, and the specific investment you select will affect your choices. For example, you may trade collectibles and real estate directly with other buyers and sellers. When you purchase stock or REITs, you may work with a **broker**. Full-service brokers generally provide more assistance with research and advice and charge higher commissions than discount brokers. Use the "Rule of Three" by comparing the costs of buying and selling with at least three firms. Other ways to make investment purchases include:

- ✦ **Direct Purchase Plans (DPPs)** or "no load" stocks are sold directly to investors. Corporations that offer stock may offer DPPs to their shareholders so they can save the cost of a broker.

- ✦ By participating in an **investment club**, you can purchase equity investments. See Unit 9 for the details.

- ✦ You can also invest via the **Internet**. Of course, the downside to online trading is "no handholding." In addition, online investors need to be very careful typing in their order. A careless extra zero (e.g., 100 shares instead of 10) can cost you plenty. Online brokerage firms will generally execute trades of reasonable amounts in excess of an investor's account balance. It is assumed that investors will "settle up" within three business days as per current Securities and Exchange Commission (SEC) regulations.

The process for executing an online trade is as follows:

1. First, you need a computer with a modem and an Internet service provider.
2. Once connected, log onto the Web site of one of the more than 100 online brokerage firms such as Accutrade, Bull & Bear, Datek, E*Trade, Fidelity, Schwab, and Web Street.
3. Then, complete an online application and send by U.S. mail additional forms and a check to open an online trading account. The minimum amount required by most online brokerage firms to establish an account is between $2,000 and $15,000.
4. Investors are then notified by e-mail when their application is received and they are approved to start making online transactions. Stock trades are generally executed within seconds of placing an order.

Diversification

Whatever investments you make, remember diversification. You can either select investments, such as mutual funds, that invest in a variety of securities, or you can purchase a variety of securities yourself. If you do it yourself, be sure to invest in different sectors of the market (e.g., energy, financial services, consumer cyclicals) as well as in different specific investments.

Summary

Equity investing means becoming a partial owner of a company or piece of property through the purchase of investments such as stock, equity mutual funds, and real estate. Capital appreciation over time is the primary objective, although some equity investments, such as REITs and equity-income mutual funds, also provide dependable dividend income. This unit has reviewed general characteristics of equity investments and "nitty gritty" details like how to purchase them. Diversification and asset allocation as they relate to equity investing were also discussed. The unit concluded with a discussion of specific equity investments. It is now time for you to consider appropriate equity investments that mesh with personal financial goals. Complete the action steps and use the Equity Investment Comparison Worksheet to make investment decisions.

Equity Investment Comparison Worksheet

Characteristic	Equity Investment #1	Equity Investment #2	Equity Investment #3
Rate of Return (recent or projected)			
Maturity Date, if any			
Minimum Initial Investment			
Minimum Subsequent Investment			
Tax Advantages, if any			
Frequency of Dividend/ Capital Gain Payouts			
Other Features:			

Action Steps

✔ Take action now.
Ownership Investing

Check off the steps after you have completed them.

❑   Make a list of financial goals so you can match them with appropriate equity and other investments.

❑   Read about equity investments in "the financial press" (e.g., business page of local paper).

❑   Investigate equity investments (e.g., stock funds) available through employer plans [e.g., 401(k)].

❑   Obtain additional investment information from Cooperative Extension or financial services firms.

❑   Identify equity investments that match your goals and available cash flow.

❑   Research these investments and compare at least three specific products (e.g., stocks).

❑   Reduce household expenses to free up money to invest.

❑   Calculate the percentage of your portfolio allocated to equity investments.

References

Brennan, P. Q. (1997). *Buying stocks without a broker*. Rutgers Cooperative Extension curriculum.

Case, S. (1994). *The first book of investing*. Rocklin, CA: Prima Publishing.

Garman, E. T. & Forgue, R. E. (2000). *Personal finance*. 6th Edition. Boston: Houghton Mifflin Company.

Gruber, B. (1996). *The investing kit*. Chicago: Dearborn Financial Publishing.

Keown, A. J. (2000, June). *Personal finance: Turning money into wealth*. 2nd Edition. Upper Saddle River, NJ: Prentice Hall.

Korn, D. (1999, March). Going from the dogs. *Financial Planning*, 73–76.

O'Neill, B. (1999). *Investing on a shoestring*. Chicago: Dearborn Financial Publishing.

Rankin, D. (1994). *Investing on your own*. Yonkers, NY: Consumer Reports Books.

Reinhardt, C., Werba, A., & Bowen, J. (1996). *The prudent investor's guide to beating the market*. Chicago: Irwin Professional Publishing.

Rosefsky, R. S. (2001, June). *Personal finance*. 8th Edition. New York: John Wiley & Sons.

Tobias, A. (1998). *The only investment guide you'll ever need*. San Diego: Harcourt Brace.

Wall, G. (1995). *The way to invest*. New York: Owl Books.

Wessel, D. (1999, March 15). U.S. stock holdings rose 20% in 1998, highest percent of assets in postwar era. *The Wall Street Journal*, A6.

Author Profile

Irene Leech, Ph.D., CFCS, is an Associate Professor of Consumer Affairs at Virginia Tech and former consumer education extension specialist. She teaches in the undergraduate and graduate resource management program at Virginia Tech. Her professional memberships include the Association for Financial Counseling and Planning Education and the American Council on Consumer Interests.

Fixed-Income Investing

— Barbara O'Neill, Ph.D., CFP, Rutgers Cooperative Extension —

I n Unit 4, you explored characteristics of equity investments such as real estate and stock. This unit will discuss general characteristics of fixed-income securities and describe 15 specific types of these investments. There are two general categories of investments: **ownership** and **loanership**. With "ownership" assets, investors own all or part of an asset (e.g., real estate, corporation). They buy shares of company stock or growth mutual funds or, perhaps, a rental property. In other words, as an owner, they have an equity or ownership interest in a company or property, and their principal and investment earnings fluctuate with market conditions and other factors (e.g., company earnings) that affect an asset's selling price.

Fixed-income investments, on the other hand, are "loanership" assets; investors loan their money to a government entity (e.g., state), corporation, or financial institution (e.g., bank, credit union) and receive interest on a regular basis (e.g., monthly, semi-annually). The rate of interest paid can either be fixed for the life of an investment (e.g., Treasury securities) or can fluctuate with the general movement of interest rates (e.g., Series EE savings bonds). The principal (amount of original investment) is returned at maturity (the date on which principal must be repaid), although its value can fluctuate (if sold beforehand) according to changes in interest rates. For many fixed-income securities (e.g., bonds), as interest rates rise, asset prices decline and, as interest rates decline, asset prices rise. This inverse relationship of interest rates and asset value, called **interest rate risk**, affects the value of fixed-income securities if you have to sell them prior to maturity. In other words, you could lose principal if interest rates rise and you have to sell early.

Why Buy Fixed-Income Investments?

There are many reasons to consider fixed-income investments. One is that they add diversification to an investor's portfolio. Research by several Nobel prize-winning economists found that, for every level of investment risk, there is a "best combination" of assets that produces the highest rate of return. Investing in just one asset class (e.g., stock, bonds, or cash), however, is less desirable than selecting a combination of assets, because doing so increases investment risk. It's like the old saying, "Don't put all of your eggs in one basket." By combining investments that are affected differently by economic events, investment risk is reduced. While both

stocks and bonds often are similarly affected by interest rates in the short run today, over the long term they have had a relatively low relationship to each other. The technical word for this is **correlation**, which is a statistical term that indicates the degree to which the movement of one variable (in this case, an asset class price) is related to another.

Besides diversification, there are several other reasons to consider fixed-income securities. First, they are a good option for conservative investors who are fearful of ownership assets. If the price fluctuations of the stock market are likely to cause sleepless nights, fixed-income investments like bonds are less risky, because investors are less likely to lose principal. Most fixed-income securities also provide a predictable stream of income. This can be an advantage for current or near retirees who seek regular income to supplement a pension and/or Social Security.

Predictability of investment return is a third feature of fixed-income securities. The rate of return is fixed for the life of most investments, and a certain amount of income can be counted upon (e.g., a 6% interest rate on a $1,000 corporate bond will pay $30 semi-annually). Some fixed-income investments also provide tax advantages. Fixed annuities, for example, are tax-deferred, and municipal bond interest is federally tax-exempt. Some investments (e.g., bond funds) also allow investors to reinvest earnings, plus most fixed-income securities typically earn a higher return than bank accounts. This is especially true for **substandard grade bonds** rated less than Baa by Moody's or BBB by Standard & Poor's. Investment yields generally increase as the credit quality of a bond issuer drops. Thus, investors can increase their income by purchasing lower-rated bonds. Further information about bond ratings is available in many public libraries. Fixed-income securities with longer maturities (e.g., 30-year bonds) typically pay a higher interest rate than shorter-term investments (e.g., ten-year bonds) to compensate investors for having their money "tied up" for additional years and for increased exposure to price fluctuations caused by interest rate risk.

Some fixed-income securities also have **capital gain** (or loss) potential. Capital gains can accrue if investments are sold in secondary markets at a premium (more than their face value) prior to maturity. Gains occur when interest rates decrease and bond prices rise. A final feature of fixed-income investments is affordability. Most investment products in this category require a minimum purchase of $1,000 or less. Treasury bills and notes, for example, both require minimum initial deposits of $1,000, as do corporate bonds, unit investment trusts (UITs), and many bond mutual funds. Even among municipal bonds, which generally require $5,000, some issuers offer $100 or $500 "minibonds" that provide tax-exempt income to small investors. Ginnie Maes, which require $25,000 to purchase directly, can be bought in $1,000 units through Unit Investment Trusts (UITs). Series EE bonds can be purchased for as little as $25 and I bonds for $50.

Next, we will briefly examine 15 fixed-income investments and five general tips for fixed-income investing. The list begins with securities sold at banks, followed by various types of bonds and other fixed-income investments generally sold by brokers.

SUBSTANDARD GRADE (A.K.A., "JUNK") BOND
Bond rated below the top four grades by a rating service such as Moody's and Standard & Poor's. They generally provide a higher return than investment grade securities to compensate investors for an increased risk of default.

CAPITAL GAINS DISTRIBUTION
Payment to investors of profits realized upon the sale of securities.

Certificates of Deposit (CDs)

Also known as "time deposits," certificates of deposit (CDs) are an insured bank product that pays a fixed rate of interest for a specified period of time (e.g., 18 months). Typical CD maturities range from seven days to five years, with higher rates of return paid on CDs with longer maturities. A penalty is assessed if funds are withdrawn prior to maturity, resulting in the loss of a certain number of days of interest (the amount varies among financial institutions). If an early withdrawal penalty exceeds the interest earned, the difference will be deducted from an investor's principal.

Many people think that CDs can only be purchased at banks. Many credit unions and full-service brokerage firms also sell federally insured CDs to investors. Investment firms purchase the CDs of banks nationwide in large blocks and sell them to investors in small denominations. The difference between their buying and selling price, called "the spread," is how they make a profit. Since brokers shop the entire country for high yields, brokered CDs often pay more attractive rates than CDs at local banks. CDs can be redeemed prior to maturity, often without penalty, but, due to interest rate risk, the value of a brokered CD can be higher or lower than someone's initial investment.

Another relatively new type of CD is the equity-indexed CD. Sold through both banks and brokers, these CDs base returns, in part, on appreciation of a stock market index like the Standard & Poor's 500 (S&P 500). Many require a $5,000 initial investment ($2,000 for IRAs). Unfortunately, equity-indexed CDs rarely include the full appreciation potential of the S&P 500, because they exclude the portion derived from company dividends. Many also cap the maximum growth rate, which further reduces upside potential. As a result, most financial advisors suggest avoiding these CDs and buying regular CDs for income and a stock index fund for capital growth.

Series EE and Series I U.S. Bonds

U.S. savings bonds are the lowest-denomination securities issued by the federal government. Income earned is exempt from state and local taxes. Federal taxes can be deferred for up to 30 years or until the owner cashes a bond. Both the Series EE and I bond are available at most banks and many credit unions and other financial institutions in denominations ranging from $50 to $10,000. Many employers offer both Series EE and inflation-adjusted I bonds through convenient payroll savings plans. The purchase price of EE bonds is one-half their face value (e.g., $50 for a $100 bond). I bonds are sold at face value in the same denominations as Series EE. The accrued interest on both series is paid when the bonds are redeemed. Bonds can be redeemed at most financial institutions.

Notes

Series EE and Series I bonds can also be purchased regularly through the U.S. Savings Bonds EasySaver plan, a savings program that automatically debits your bank account on a schedule you determine. EasySaver information is available by calling toll-free 1-877-811-SAVE (7283) or by downloading an enrollment form from <www.easysaver.gov>. Small business owners can give EasySaver information to their employees to help them save without the need to administer a payroll deduction plan. Call toll free 1-877-811-SAVE and mention key 11 to obtain EasySaver information for small business owners.

Series EE and Series I bonds must be held six months before being eligible for redemption. Redemptions prior to five years from issue are subject to a three-month interest penalty (e.g., 21 months of interest for a bond cashed in after 24 months). Redemption values are available using the tables and Savings Bonds Wizard software available free at the Treasury Department Web site, <www.savingsbonds.gov> or by consulting tables available at most banks, credit unions, and other financial institutions. You may also request a free table by writing to Bureau of the Public Debt, Savings Bond Operations Office, Parkersburg, WV 26106-1328.

Series EE bonds issued since May 1997 pay an interest rate based on 90% of the average market yield of five-year Treasury securities. These rates are adjusted twice a year on May 1 and November 1 based on Treasury yields during the preceding six months. Series I bonds earn a fixed rate over and above an inflation adjustment based upon changes in the Consumer Price Index. Interest accrues federally tax-deferred for as long as 30 years or until the bond is redeemed. Earnings on both series are subject to federal tax, but may be tax-free if cashed in a year when the owner pays qualified higher education expenses. Income limits and other restrictions apply; see IRS Form 8815 for details. Earnings from all savings bonds are exempt from state and local taxes. Current rate information can be obtained by phoning 1-800-4US-BOND (1-800-487-2663).

It is sometimes confusing to determine the current redemption value of Series EE bonds or when they have doubled in value. If interest rates are so low that a bond is not worth its face value in 17 years, the U.S. Treasury will add a one-time "make-up" to ensure that it is worth twice as much as an investor paid (e.g., $50 for a EE bond originally purchased for $25). Basic bond redemption tables are free and available at many banks or from the Bureau of the Public Debt (see above). Another way to determine the value of a Series EE bond is to use the Savings Bond Wizard feature of the Treasury Department's Web site at <www.savingsbonds.gov>. If your grandmother gave you a savings bond 20 years ago, for example, you can check a table or the Web site to find what it is worth.

There is also another U.S. savings bond available to investors: HH bonds. HH bonds are issued at full face value through an exchange of EE bonds, thus deferring federal income tax due on EE bond earnings for as long as 20 additional years. Denominations range from $500 to $10,000 and interest is paid semi-annually.

Money Market Mutual Funds

Money market mutual funds are a type of mutual fund consisting of high-quality, short-term debt instruments such as Treasury bills and short-term corporate IOUs. Like all mutual funds, money market mutual fund (MMMF) portfolios are professionally managed, and a management fee is charged against fund assets to cover this expense. MMMFs offer market-based rates and are quick to respond to changing conditions, because the average maturity of securities in their portfolio is 90 days or less. The minimum initial deposit is set by individual investment firms and can range from $250 to $25,000. MMMFs can be purchased directly from investment companies or with the assistance of financial advisors.

Unlike bank-sponsored money market deposit accounts (MMDAs), there is no FDIC insurance if a MMMF fails to maintain a $1 share price. Failures have happened very infrequently in the last 20 years, however, and most investment firms have shored up MMMF prices with other company assets to avoid a loss of principal by investors. Limited check writing is generally available on MMMFs with a minimum amount (e.g., $250) per check. Investors seeking both safety of principal and tax advantages can select tax-exempt MMMFs that include short-term securities issued by state and local governments. Other conservative choices are MMMFs that invest solely in Treasury bills and/or Treasuries plus debt of federal government agencies.

Bonds: An Overview

Before discussing various types of bonds, some background is in order. Bonds are debts or IOUs of corporations or government entities. Bond issuers promise to pay a specified rate of interest, called a coupon rate, periodically and to repay the face (a.k.a., par) value of the bond (e.g., $1,000) at maturity. Corporate and municipal bonds are typically sold by brokers, who receive a sales commission. Bonds are subject to **interest rate risk**. If interest rates rise, the value of previously issued bonds will drop as investors demand a price adjustment equivalent to earning the prevailing interest rate. If interest rates drop, a previously issued bond will be worth more than its face value because investors would be willing to pay a premium to obtain a bond paying more than the currently available rate. The value of long-term bonds is affected more than short-term bonds by interest rate fluctuations. Bonds are also subject to **call risk**. This means that a bond issuer may choose to retire existing bonds, issued when interest rates were high, and reissue them with new debt at a lower interest rate.

The capacity of bond issuers to repay their debt is rated by various commercial firms such as Moody's and Standard & Poor's. Bonds rated Baa to Aaa by Moody's and BBB to AAA by Standard & Poor's are considered **investment grade**. Those with lower ratings are termed substandard grade. Substandard grade bonds or bond funds can often be recognized by the words "junk" or "high yield" in their title.

MATURITY
The date on which the principal amount of a bond, investment contract, or loan must be repaid.
INVESTMENT-GRADE BOND
Bond rated with one of the top four grades by a rating service like Moody's and Standard & Poor's, indicating a high level of creditworthiness.

U.S. Treasury Securities

Treasury securities are an obligation of the U.S. government and are considered the safest of all debt instruments because there has never been a default in payment. This concept is sometimes stated with the words "full faith and credit of the U.S. government." Treasury securities are sold at periodic government auctions, with fewer issues being sold recently because of the shrinking federal deficit. They are exempt from state and local income taxes due to the principal of **reciprocal immunity**. This means that the federal government doesn't tax state and local debt (e.g., municipal bonds) and state and local governments don't tax federal debt (e.g., Treasury Securities).

There are two types of Treasury securities currently available: bills and notes. Both require a $1,000 minimum deposit with larger amounts purchased in increments of $1,000. **Treasury bills** have the shortest term of all Treasury securities and come in three- and six-month maturities. They are purchased at a **discount** with investors paying $1,000 or more up front and receiving back an amount, called "the discount," equal to the interest rate determined by the most recent auction. At maturity, an investor's original purchase amount (principal) is returned. If interest rates are 4%, for example, an investor with $1,000 would receive a discount of $40 ($1,000 x 0.04) shortly after purchase and their $1,000 principal back at maturity.

Treasury notes currently come with two-, five-, and ten-year maturities. They pay a fixed rate of interest semi-annually until maturity, when investors get their principal back. For example, a $1,000, five-year Treasury note with a 5% yield pays $25 every six months ($50 per year). The yield on Treasury notes is generally higher than that of bills to compensate for the risk of investing longer and the greater volatility that accompanies interest-rate changes.

Treasury securities can be purchased from a bank or brokerage firm for a fee of about $50 or with no fee from the Federal Reserve Bank's "Treasury Direct" program. An application, called a tender form, is required and can be obtained by calling 202-874-4000 for a list of Federal Reserve Banks or through the Treasury Department Web site <www.publicdebt.treas.gov>. With Treasury Direct, an investor must specify a bank account where their interest payments can be deposited electronically. Treasury securities also can be sold through the Treasury Direct program for a nominal charge.

Municipal Bonds

Municipal bonds are debt instruments of state and local governments or government-related entities (e.g., bridge or highway authorities). **General obligation (GO) bonds** are backed by the full taxing ability of the issuer and are considered the safest of municipal bonds. A second type of municipal bond, the **revenue bond**, is backed by some type of revenue-generating source (e.g., fares, tolls, fees) and generally pays a slightly higher rate of return.

Municipal bonds are attractive to persons in the 27% (decreasing to 26% in 2004–2005 and 25% in 2006) marginal tax bracket and higher. Even though municipal bonds pay a lower return than other bonds, investors keep more of what they earn because the interest is generally federally tax-exempt. Interest is also state tax-exempt, if bonds are issued by an investor's state of residence. An exception is the so-called private purpose municipal bond sold to finance sports stadiums, airports, hospitals, and the like. Municipal bonds are generally sold by brokerage firms in $5,000 increments with less expensive "minibonds" requiring a lower amount (e.g., $500). Interest is paid semi-annually. Investors can also obtain the tax advantages of a municipal bond by purchasing a municipal bond mutual fund, often for an initial investment of $1,000 or less.

Corporate Bonds

Corporate bonds are debt instruments issued by for-profit companies to raise capital for expansion and/or ongoing operations. They are generally sold in $1,000 increments and pay taxable interest twice a year. Corporate bonds generally pay higher interest rates than government bonds with comparable credit ratings and maturities. Investing in a corporation is a greater risk than a government entity that has the ability to raise revenue through taxes. Thus, investors must be compensated accordingly. The least risky of all corporate bonds is a **mortgage bond,** because it is backed by a company's land and buildings. Bonds backed by non-real estate assets (e.g., airplanes, securities) have more risk. The highest risk corporate bond is a **debenture**, which is a corporate bond backed only by a company's future earnings and promise to repay. Conservative investors will want to select mortgage bonds issued by investment grade (i.e., highly rated) companies.

Convertible Bonds

As their name suggests, convertible bonds are a type of corporate bond that allows investors to "have their cake and eat it, too"—almost. They provide the upside potential of stocks (the opportunity to participate in company earnings) with the downside protection of bonds (a fixed return and repayment of principal at maturity). Convertible bonds can be exchanged for a specified number of shares of common stock of the issuing company. As the price of the company stock increases, the convertible bond price also increases, because the option to convert becomes more valuable. This correlation is true whether an investor chooses to convert or not. The tradeoff is that convertible bonds generally convert to fewer shares of stock than you could buy for the cost of a bond. Almost all convertible bonds are callable. Even though they are a "hybrid" investment, convertibles (like all bonds) are sensitive to interest rate fluctuations. They can be purchased as individual securities in $1,000 increments or through convertible bond mutual funds.

Notes

Zero-Coupon Bonds

As their name implies, zero-coupon bonds pay no (zero) annual interest. Instead, they are sold at a deep discount and eventually grow to full face value ($1,000). An investor might pay only $200 or $300, for example, for a bond that matures in 15 or 20 years. Brokers may require a $5,000 purchase, however, or five times the initial cost. For example, an 8% zero-coupon bond with 15 years to maturity would cost $308. To purchase five such bonds ($5,000 face value) would cost $1,540 (5 x $308). So, in this example, if you invest $1,540 now, you know you'll get back $5,000 in 15 years. This return might be suitable for a goal you want to achieve in 15 years (e.g., future education expenses of a young child).

Many investors like zero-coupon bonds for their relatively low upfront cost and predictability. An investor knows exactly how much they'll have at maturity. Two disadvantages of zero-coupon bonds are their extreme volatility with interest rate changes and the fact that annual increases in value are considered taxable income. Immediate taxation can be avoided, however, by using zero-coupon bonds for tax-deferred retirement plans, such as IRAs, or by buying tax-exempt (e.g., municipal) zero-coupon municipal bonds.

Unit Investment Trusts

Unit Investment Trusts (UITs) are a professionally selected portfolio of similar securities (e.g., 30-year municipal bonds) packaged together and sold by brokerage firms. Unlike mutual funds, UITs are a "buy and hold" investment, and there is no ongoing portfolio management. UIT sponsors simply buy a collection of bonds (and, with some UITs, stocks) and hold them. Investors receive periodic interest payments and a return of principal at maturity. If bonds within a UIT portfolio are sold or called prior to maturity, some principal may be returned sooner.

UITs are generally sold in $1,000 increments called units. The interest earned is taxable unless a UIT invests in tax-exempt bonds. If an investor needs his/her money prior to maturity, units can be redeemed at their current market value, subject to interest rate risk. Two advantages of UITs are broad diversification and steady cash flow. A specified rate of return is locked in for the duration of a UIT. Two disadvantages are high upfront costs (typically a 3% to 5% sales charge) and the potential for loss if units are sold prior to maturity. For some UITs, selling units prior to maturity may be difficult or costly, because secondary markets are small. For more information on UITs, see Unit 8.

Bond Mutual Funds

Instead of purchasing individual securities, an investor might decide to purchase shares of a bond mutual fund. Advantages include broad diversification, liquidity, and ongoing professional management. In addition, bond fund accounts can sometimes be opened for $500 or less, making them attractive for persons with small dollar amounts to invest. The biggest disadvantage of bond mutual funds is that,

unlike individual securities and UITs, there is no fixed maturity date. Thus, the price of shares is always subject to fluctuation with changes in interest rates, and an investor could lose principal if interest rates increase. As with all mutual funds, the key factors to look for when selecting a bond fund are historical performance and expenses. Unlike stock funds, that have the potential for capital appreciation to offset fund expenses, bond funds must rely on low management costs to enhance their returns. In addition, bond funds generally invest in similar securities (e.g., Treasuries), so most of the difference in return among bond funds is due to differences in cost. The average annual **expense ratio** (expenses as a percentage of fund assets) for bond funds is about 1% ($1 for every $100 invested), but there are some low-cost fund families like Vanguard, T. Rowe Price, TIAA-CREF, and Fidelity that charge significantly less.

A 1997 study of bond mutual funds by *Consumer Reports* magazine found that, among government bond funds, funds with low expense ratios outperformed their peers. One low-cost bond mutual fund is a bond index fund. Bond index funds purchase the same securities that comprise a benchmark bond index, such as the Lehman Brothers Aggregate. Since the portfolio of securities is predetermined by whatever bonds comprise an index, trading costs are minimal and bond index fund management expenses are low. Like individual bonds, bond funds with the longest maturities are extremely volatile when interest rates fluctuate. Conservative investors should select short-term bond funds consisting of investment-grade securities.

Mortgage-Backed Securities

Mortgage-backed securities are investments in a portfolio of home mortgages and are sometimes referred to as "pass-through" securities, because homeowners' mortgage principal and interest payments are "passed through" to investors. The most well-known mortgage-backed security is the **Ginnie Mae**, which is issued by the Government National Mortgage Association (GNMA). Ginnie Maes carry the "full faith and credit" guarantee of the federal government. Ginnie Maes require a $25,000 minimum purchase, with $5,000 increments, from brokers, but can also be purchased indirectly for $1,000 through units in a Ginnie Mae unit investment trust. They can also be purchased through mutual funds that invest in U.S. government agency securities (minimum amounts vary per fund).

Two other mortgage-backed securities that are not backed by the federal government are **Freddie Macs**, issued by the Federal Home Loan Mortgage Corporation (FHLMC) and **Fannie Maes**, issued by the Federal National Mortgage Association (FNMA). They also require $25,000 and typically pay a higher rate than Ginnie Maes to compensate investors for the extra risk of not being government-insured.

The biggest disadvantages of all three mortgage-backed securities are an uncertain maturity and irregular monthly payments. Although the mortgages in their portfolios are issued for 30 years, the average life of a mortgage-backed security

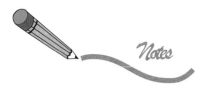
Notes

is only ten to 12 years, because homeowners frequently move or refinance. Also, if investors spend the part of their monthly check that is a return of principal instead of reinvesting it, they will have nothing left when the last mortgage in their Ginnie Mae portfolio is repaid.

Collateralized Mortgage Obligations

Collateralized mortgage obligations (CMOs) are another type of mortgage-backed security. CMOs were developed to address investors' concern about receiving income from other mortgage-backed securities in unpredictable increments. With CMOs, the portfolio of mortgages is divided into various classes, called **tranches**, thus offering investors a choice of estimated maturity dates to match financial goals. Investors in a particular tranche typically receive semi-annual interest payments that differ from period-to-period and from other tranches. Tranches with a longer maturity generally pay a higher return to compensate investors for incurring greater interest rate risk. The principal portion of mortgage payments corresponding to all tranches goes to investors in a single tranche until that tranche is retired. Each tranche gets its principal back when all the tranches before it have been repaid. CMOs are available in $1,000 increments through brokerage firms and pay a higher yield than comparable mortgage-backed securities. Two disadvantages are their complexity and the fact that principal prepayment can still come sooner (or later) than expected. Just as with other mortgage-backed securities, investors must realize that principal is being repaid throughout the life of a CMO, not at maturity like bonds. Investors who mistakenly think that CMO payments are just interest may inadvertently spend their principal.

Annuities

An annuity is a contract with an insurance company to provide regular income immediately or at some time in the future for a specified period (e.g., the lifetime of an annuitant or an annuitant and his/her spouse), typically during retirement years. In return, an investor deposits a sum of money with an insurance company, which grows tax-deferred until withdrawal, or makes periodic payments. There are two types of annuities: **variable annuities,** which provide access to growth-oriented (ownership) and income-oriented (loanership) investments through a choice of mutual fund subaccounts, and **fixed annuities,** which guarantee a fixed rate of return for a specified period of time. Thus, fixed annuities are like a CD, but are tax-deferred. A rate of return is locked in for a period of one to five years after purchase and then adjusted annually according to market conditions. Annuities generally require a $5,000 minimum investment. Annuity investors should compare surrender charges (a fee assessed for cashing out early), rates of return, and the financial health of insurance companies that offer annuities. Be sure to check with rating services such as A.M. Best, Moody's, and Duff and Phelps, and stick with top-rated insurance companies.

Preferred Stock

Although technically a form of stock, preferred stock is often listed as a fixed-income investment, because it behaves more like a bond, but has no fixed maturity date. The word "preferred" refers to the fact that shareholders receive preferential treatment. They are paid dividends before common stock shareholders and, in the event of a corporate liquidation, can claim corporate assets after bondholders but before common stock shareholders. Preferred stock typically pays a fixed dividend rate similar to the coupon rate on a bond. Share prices fluctuate inversely with changes in interest rates. Par value on preferred stock is usually about $25 per share, so a round lot (100 shares) would cost $2,500. Dividends paid are a fixed percentage of par value. Preferred stock shares are available through brokerage firms.

Guaranteed Investment Contracts

Called GICs for short, guaranteed investment contracts are fixed-income contracts issued by insurance companies as an investment option for 401(k) retirement plans. Another more commonly used name for GICs is "stable value funds." Like CDs, only tax-deferred, GICs pay a fixed-interest rate for a specified period of time (e.g., three to five years). Because they are backed by an insurance company and not the federal government, GICs generally pay a higher return than CDs and other cash investments. Their return is lower than stocks, however, leading to criticism that they are inappropriate for long-term financial goals like retirement.

Five Tips For Fixed-Income Investors

1. **Know the risks.** All investments have risks, including fixed-income securities. To earn a higher return, for example, an investor may need to consider bonds from a less creditworthy issuer.

2. **Beware of guarantees.** Even with a portfolio of Treasury securities, an investor can lose money via interest rate risk. Beware of promises that "you can never lose principal." You can.

3. **Ladder your portfolio.** Stagger the purchase of bonds, CDs, and Treasury securities to spread out the tax owed and expose only a portion of your portfolio to interest rate changes at any one time.

4. **Use bonds to hedge stock investments.** Have your cake and eat it, too. Buy a zero-coupon bond to guarantee the return of principal and use the balance of principal to invest in ownership assets (e.g., stock).

5. **Match investments with financial goals.** Invest with a goal in mind. For example, use a two-year Treasury note for an upcoming car purchase or an eight-year zero-coupon bond for a child's education.

Summary

Fixed-income investments involve loaning money for a period of time in exchange for periodic interest. Income is the primary objective, and some investments also have growth potential if sold for a premium prior to maturity. This unit has reviewed characteristics of 15 specific fixed-income investment products, including advantages, disadvantages, and required minimum investments. Now you need to consider appropriate fixed-income investments that mesh with your personal financial goals. Complete the action steps listed below and use the Fixed-Income Investment Comparison Worksheet to make investment decisions.

Fixed-Income Investment Comparison Worksheet

Characteristic	Fixed-Income Investment #1	Fixed-Income Investment #2	Fixed-Income Investment #3
Rate of Return			
Maturity Date, if any			
Minimum Investment Amount			
Subsequent Investment Amount			
Tax Advantages, if any			
Frequency of Interest Payments			
Other Features			

Action Steps

✔ Take action now.
Fixed-Income Investing

Check off the steps after you have completed them.

- ❑ Identify fixed-income investments that match your goals and available cash flow.

- ❑ Research these investments and compare at least three specific products (e.g., bond mutual funds). Make a list of financial goals so you can match them with appropriate fixed-income and other investments.

- ❑ Determine your marginal tax bracket to see if tax-exempt investments are a cost-effective option (see Unit 7 for details).

- ❑ Investigate fixed-income investments (e.g., bond funds) available through your employer [e.g., 401(k) plan].

- ❑ Attend an investment seminar sponsored by Cooperative Extension or financial services firms.

- ❑ Reduce household expenses to free up money to invest (see Unit 3 for details).

- ❑ Calculate the percentage of your portfolio allocated to fixed-income investments.

References

Bond fund expenses: Vanguard rules the roost (1996, Dec.). *Mutual Funds*, 33.

Bond mutual funds (1998). Washington DC: Investment Company Institute.

Goetting, M. (1998). *Investing in certificates of deposit*. Montana State University Extension Service Fact Sheet MT9801.

Matejic, D. (1995). *Using U.S. savings bonds to reach financial goals*. Rutgers Cooperative Extension Fact Sheet #FS807.

O'Neill, B. (1998, Oct.). Are Treasuries worth a second look? *NAPFA Advisor*, 36–42.

Pederson, D. J. (1997). *U.S. savings bonds*. Detroit, MI: TSBI Publishing.

Rankin, D. 1994. *Investing on your own*. Yonkers, NY: Consumer Reports Books.

Reinhardt, C., Werba, A., & Bowen, J. (1996). *The prudent investor's guide to beating the market*. Chicago: Irwin Publishing.

The fundamentals of fixed-income investing (1991). Baltimore: T. Rowe Price Co.

Who needs a bond fund? (1997, Sept.). *Consumer Reports*, 41–44.

Zwieg, J. (1998, June). Don't believe the bull: Bond funds do have a place. *Money*, 63–64.

Author Profile

Barbara O'Neill, Ph.D., holds the rank of full professor in the Family & Consumer Sciences Department at Cook College, Rutgers University. She has been a family and consumer sciences educator in Sussex County, New Jersey, since 1978 and is a certified financial planner (CFP), an accredited financial counselor (AFC), and a certified housing counselor (CHC). Dr. O'Neill has written over 1,500 consumer newspaper articles and over 100 articles and abstracts for professional journals and conference proceedings. She is also the author of four books, two financial case-study books published by Rutgers University, and *Saving On A Shoestring* and *Investing On A Shoestring*, trade books published by Dearborn Financial Publishing.

Mutual Fund INVESTING

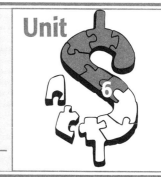

Patricia Q. Brennan, M.A., CFP, Rutgers Cooperative Extension

Notes

In Units 4 and 5 you learned how to purchase individual securities such as stocks and bonds. Another popular investment choice is mutual funds. In 1979, mutual fund industry assets totaled $56 billion. By 2001, they stood at $7 trillion! In January 2001, the Investment Company Institute reported over 8,000 mutual funds (over 12,000 if you count different share classes). According to the Securities and Exchange Commission (SEC), the number of American households that own mutual funds rose from one in 18 in 1980 to almost one in two by 2000, and just under half of adult Americans invested in the stock market, directly or indirectly through mutual funds and retirement plans, by 2000—up from 21.1% in 1990. Yet, a survey conducted by the Investment Company Institute, the mutual fund industry's trade group, continues to show that, although more than 77 million Americans own funds, most investors do not understand what they own or how they work.

Almost everyone has a need to learn the basics of mutual funds. Some might need to know how to choose investments for a 401(k) or other retirement plan, others how to invest money received from an insurance or divorce settlement. Many people just want to know how to get started as an investor. Still others own a hodge-podge of funds bought at various times without much thought as to how they complement each other. Getting a year-end bonus, a tax refund, or reading that a popular mutual fund is about to close also prompts many would-be investors to buy a fund.

An individual's investment portfolio should be more than just a collection of mutual funds. Before you select funds to invest in, you will want to determine your investment goals, your time-frame for needing the money, and the amount of risk you are willing to take. This unit will help you learn how to invest in one of the best investment vehicles ever created *in the context of your own overall financial plan.* One of the top reasons for learning about mutual funds is that you can save money if you choose the funds and maintain your portfolio yourself.

What is a Mutual Fund?

A **mutual fund** is a portfolio of stocks, bonds, or other securities that is collectively owned by hundreds or thousands of investors and managed by a professional investment company. The shareholders are people who have similar investment goals.

Unit 6 • Mutual Fund Investing   71

Each fund has specific investment criteria, which are spelled out in its **prospectus**, the official booklet that describes the mutual fund. Investors then know what they are getting and can match their objective to that of a fund. The pooled money has more buying power than one investor alone, so that a fund can own hundreds of different securities. Thus, its success is not dependent on how just one or two companies perform.

A mutual fund makes money in several ways, including by earning dividends or interest on the investments it owns and by selling securities that have appreciated in value. You, in turn, make money in the form of dividends and interest that are passed on to you and the increase (or decrease) in the fund's value. The mutual fund manager keeps constant watch on financial markets and adjusts the portfolio to achieve the strongest returns. By owning part of a fund, the hard work of selecting and monitoring stocks and bonds is done for you.

The majority of mutual funds available are **open-end** funds, which are the focus of this unit. Open-end funds can have an unlimited number of investors or money in the fund. Managers of **closed-end** funds, on the other hand, decide up front how many shares they will issue and when they will sell them. The only way to purchase shares in a closed-end fund, once the original shares have been sold, is to buy them from a current investor. Occasionally, open-end funds can and do close to new investors, often because of high cash inflows that cannot be invested in a timely manner. They do not become closed-end funds, however, because current shareholders can still buy additional shares from the fund company.

When investors purchase a mutual fund, they own a piece of an investment portfolio. They share in the gains, losses, and expenses in proportion to the amount they have invested in the fund. At the close of every trading day, a mutual fund company tallies the value of all the securities in its portfolio and deducts its expenses (e.g., management fees, administrative expenses, advertising costs). The balance is divided by the number of shares owned by shareholders to arrive at the dollar value of one share of the mutual fund. This value, the **net asset value** or NAV, is the price your fund pays you per share when you sell. (An exception to receiving NAV at sale time is back-end load funds that charge a redemption fee.)

At this point, you may want to review Units 4 and 5 to understand the underlying instruments in most mutual funds.

Why Mutual Funds Versus Individual Securities?

For a majority of people, mutual funds should be a major part of their investment portfolio—unless they have a lot of money and ample time to devote to investing in individual securities. While there are arguments for buying stocks and bonds directly, consider buying mutual funds first, or at least use them as a **core holding**, because of the following drawbacks to individual stock and bond picking and trading:

- First, a great deal of time and expertise is required to analyze a company—its prospects for earnings growth, its performance over the short and long term in

OPEN-END FUND
An investment company that continually buys and sells shares to meet investor demand. It can have an unlimited number of investors or money in the fund.

CLOSED-END FUND
An investment company that issues a limited number of shares that can be bought and sold on market exchanges.

CORE HOLDING
The foundation of a portfolio (e.g., a stock index fund) to which an investor might add additional securities.

comparison to its competitors, its debt level and creditworthiness, its new products in the pipeline, and technological changes looming that might harm or improve business.

- Second, purchasing individual securities involves higher transaction costs. Even when you use a discount broker, the commissions you pay to buy and sell are not cheap. (However, the cost of online trading is getting lower every year—see Unit 9.)
- Third, owning individual stocks means you are less likely to have proper diversification. To diversify a stock portfolio, you need to own at least ten to 20 different companies in different industries, which could cost thousands of dollars. For the same price you might pay for 100 shares of one security, you can buy shares in a fund that owns 100 securities. Diversification lowers your investment risk—if one or two stocks plunge, others may gain in value, offsetting the loss.

Nevertheless, there are several circumstances when you do not need mutual funds:

- If you are adept at picking individual stocks
- If you have at least $20,000–50,000 to buy at least ten to 20 stocks (depending on stock prices)
- If you plan to invest in Treasury bills or notes

In the last case, you would do better purchasing them directly through the Federal Reserve's Treasury Direct program (<www.publicdebt.treas.gov>).

Mutual Funds: Ten Advantages

1. You get **full-time, professional money management**. Most people do not have the time or skill to select and monitor individual stocks and bonds.
2. You get **reduced risk through diversification** because a mutual fund owns many stocks or bonds. You can also pick your level of market risk by choosing particular types of funds (e.g., money market funds to insure your principal will not drop in value, bond funds if you want current income and some stability in your portfolio, stock funds if you want your money to grow over the long term).
3. You will earn **competitive returns** on your investment. Mutual funds can furnish the kinds of returns you need to reach your goals. In fact, by choosing an index fund (a fund that invests in securities of one of the broadly based market indexes such as Standard and Poor's 500), you can expect to match the market's performance, minus the expenses of running the fund. This is an assurance that no other investment can provide.
4. **You don't need a lot of money to get started.** Many funds require only $1,000 to open an account, and some funds require minimum initial investments as low as $250 to $500. Subsequent deposits can be as small as $25 to $100 if an **automatic investment plan** (AIP) is adopted. An AIP is an arrangement where you agree to have money automatically withdrawn from your bank account on a regular basis, (e.g., once a month or every quarter) and used to purchase fund shares.

5. You retain **ready access to your money**. A mutual fund is required to buy back your shares, which makes withdrawals easy. It will mail your check within seven days of the request at the closing price (NAV) on the day it is received. (An exception to receiving NAV at sale time is back-end load funds that charge a redemption fee.)

6. Mutual funds are a **cheaper** way to get the investing job done. Research and operating costs are shared by the thousands of shareholders. The most efficiently run funds have an **expense ratio** (the percentage of fund assets deducted for management and operating expenses) of less than 1% a year. Some well-established funds charge annual fees as low as 0.2% to 0.5%. Also, many funds are sold directly through their sponsors with no sales charge; these are known as "no-load" funds. Funds that charge a sales commission are called "load" funds.

7. Mutual funds are **convenient**. They can be purchased (and sold) directly from a mutual fund company by mail and by telephone and from full-service brokers, financial planners, banks, or insurance companies. (*Important note: When mutual funds are purchased from banks, they are not insured by the FDIC like other bank products.*) In addition, some discount brokers have established mutual fund "supermarkets," where investors can own funds from many different fund families in one consolidated account without any sales charges or transaction fees. Earnings from mutual funds can also be automatically reinvested in additional shares. Reinvesting and compounding are keys to building wealth.

8. **Automatic withdrawal plans are available**, making it possible to have a steady stream of income for retirement (e.g., withdrawals of $250 per month).

9. Mutual funds have **less risk of bankruptcy or fraud** than many other securities, because they are highly regulated by the federal government through the SEC, which is charged with ensuring that mutual funds and investment advisors follow specific rules of disclosure.

10. **Monitoring mutual funds is simple.** Prices are reported daily in the financial section of many newspapers and more in-depth information is available in the Sunday business sections (see Unit 9 for details).

Mutual Fund Disadvantages

1. **If there is a broad market drop, your fund's value will dip with it.** The diversification of most mutual funds protects you when one or several securities fall, but not when the whole market takes a downturn. The fact that funds can fluctuate up and down, sometimes wildly, is par for the course and should not deter you from investing or scare you out of the market.

2. There is **no guaranteed rate of return** with mutual funds as there is with CDs and Treasury securities. Since risk is higher, the likelihood of greater earnings is increased. You must also expect investment performance to fluctuate.

3. **Unwanted taxable distributions** can also be a disadvantage. Funds are required to pay out 98% of their dividends, interest, and capital gains annually. Taxes must be paid on these distributions, even if you never received them but instead reinvested them in additional shares. Unfortunately, sometimes you can also owe taxes even if your fund lost money for the year. For the time being, however, this

is a non-issue, if funds are held in a tax-deferred account such as a 401(k) or IRA.

4. **Record-keeping for tax purposes can be hard work.** Investors who are not meticulous about keeping track of fund purchases and sales may end up paying higher taxes than are actually owed at the time of sale because of a miscalculation of their **cost basis**. This is the amount of your original deposit, plus additional contributions and reinvested dividends and capital gains. The amount of taxes you pay will vary depending on the method you use to calculate your gain or loss (e.g., average price, first-in, first-out, or specific identification). Thus, it is important to keep every annual statement for as long as you own the fund.

The Mutual Fund Marketplace

Mutual funds fall into three main categories:
- Stock (investing primarily in stocks)
- Bond (investing in debt issues)
- Money Market (investing in short-term cash assets)

All are established to achieve one of the following investment objectives:
- Growth
- Income
- Growth and Income
- Preservation of Capital

A mutual fund's stated objective might read something like, "This fund seeks capital appreciation," meaning it is appropriate for investors who want to grow their money over the long term. Or it could state, "this fund seeks current income," indicating that the fund should be considered by investors who need a regular stream of income from their investments. The way these objectives are to be accomplished is outlined in the fund's prospectus and is the responsibility of the professional money manager hired by the mutual fund company.

To be a successful investor, you must match your objectives to that of the fund (e.g., long-term growth for retirement in 15 years). Equally important is matching the fund's risk level to your own risk tolerance. Study the fund's objective and understand the strategies it uses to achieve its goal in light of what you want to accomplish. Refer to figure 1 on page 83 to put various categories of mutual funds into perspective according to their level of risk and return.

The worksheets that follow break down mutual fund types by their basic investment objectives. Use them to help you match your goals with the appropriate funds. Examples for each category are provided. Any of the sample objectives could be met by any of the mutual fund types in each category. Write in your goals in the space provided on the left under Your Objective in each chart.

Worksheet 1. Mutual Funds with a Growth Objective

Your Objective	Mutual Funds with a Growth Objective
Examples: Retirement in 25 years College fund for a newborn *Your Objectives:* _____ _____ _____ _____ _____ _____	**Growth funds** invest for the long term, and share prices can fluctuate considerably. They buy profitable, well-established companies that expect above-average earnings growth. Income is secondary, paying very small dividends, if any. **Aggressive growth** (also called maximum capital appreciation) funds use riskier investment techniques (e.g., options, short selling) and/or invest in stocks of smaller, less-proven companies. They can be very volatile, but the tradeoff is a high potential for capital appreciation. **Small capitalization funds** invest in stocks of small companies with assets under $1 billion and are riskier than larger capitalization stock funds (over $5 billion in assets). (Capitalization means number of shares outstanding multiplied by the price per share.) **Specialty** or **sector funds** limit investments to a specific industry (e.g., health care, biotechnology, financial services). **International funds** invest in securities of countries outside the United States. **Global funds** invest in securities worldwide, including the United States. **Index funds** invest in stocks of one of the major broadly based market indexes such as the S&P 500 (large companies), Russell 2000 (small companies), or Europe, Australia, Far East or EAFE (international). Generally, these are passively managed funds with low expenses (meaning there is no manager deciding when to buy or sell securities).

Worksheet 2. Mutual Funds with an Income Objective

Your Objective	Mutual Funds with an Income Objective
Examples: Additional income for high tax-bracket retiree. Supplement Social Security and pension for living expenses. Lower risk in a stock-rich portfolio *Your Objectives:* _____ _____ _____ _____ _____ _____	**Income funds** usually include a combination of bonds and utility stocks to produce steady income and lower investment risk. **Corporate bond funds** are available in short-term, intermediate, or long-term maturities. They invest in investment-grade bonds (debt) of seasoned companies. Investment-grade bonds have ratings of AAA, AA, A, or BBB by Moody's or Standard and Poor's. **Municipal bond funds** (short-, intermediate-, and long-term) invest in tax-exempt municipal issues of state and local governments. They are generally sought by investors above the 15% tax bracket. **High-yield (junk) bond funds** buy bonds with less than a BBB rating, thereby increasing risk to seek a higher return (not suitable for the risk-averse). See Unit 5. **Government bond funds** invest in safe government-backed securities (e.g., Treasury notes). **Ginnie Mae (GNMA) funds** hold securities backed by a pool of government-insured mortgages. **Global bond funds** invest in bonds of overseas companies.

Worksheet 3. Mutual Funds with Growth and Income Objectives

Your Objective	Mutual Funds with Growth and Income Objectives
Examples: College Tuition in 7 Years Retirement in 10 Years *Your Objectives:* _____ _____ _____	**Equity-income funds** aim for moderate income and some growth, investing primarily in blue chip companies and utilities that pay current income and higher dividends. **Growth and income funds** aim for more long-term growth and a little less income than equity-income funds. They invest in large well-known firms that pay dividends. **Balanced funds** combine stocks and bonds in one portfolio to earn a reasonable income with reasonable growth. They are usually found in a fixed ratio of 60% stocks to 40% bonds.

Worksheet 4. Mutual Funds with a Preservation of Capital Objective

Your Objective	Mutual Funds with a Preservation of Capital Objective
Examples: Down Payment on a House in 1 Year Wedding in 18 Months —Upper Rate Tax Bracket *Your Objectives:* _____ _____ _____	**Taxable and tax-free money market funds** invest in very short-term debt securities such as Treasury bills and corporate IOUs known as commercial paper. **Tax-free money market funds** invest in very short-term securities issued by state and local governments.

Worksheet 5. Mutual Funds with All Four Objectives

Your Objective	Mutual Funds with All Four Objectives
Examples: **Invest for Retirement in 5 Years in a One-Fund Portfolio** **New Graduate Starting from Scratch** *Your Objectives:* _____ _____ _____ _____ _____ _____	**Lifestyle funds** typically offer three to four portfolios from which to select one with different mixes of stocks, bonds, and cash planned to fit people at different stages in the life cycle, different tolerances for risk, or those getting started with a limited amount of money (e.g., T. Rowe Price Personal Strategy funds, Vanguard Life-Strategy funds, Dreyfus Lifetime Portfolio). **Asset allocation funds** aim for good returns with relatively low risk by combining changing amounts of the three asset classes—stocks, bonds, and cash. Managers of the fund shift the investment portfolio among the categories at their own discretion. **Funds of funds** are mutual funds that buy shares of other funds. In some instances they are run by a mutual fund family (e.g., Vanguard STAR, composed of nine Vanguard stock, bond, and money market funds; T. Rowe Price Spectrum-Income or Spectrum-Growth, composed of six bond and six stock funds, respectively).

What Mutual Funds Cost and Where to Buy Them

What you pay to purchase or sell a mutual fund, as well as the ongoing fund operating expenses, can have a great impact on the rate of return on your investments. So, keeping fees to a minimum is in your best interest. Generally, there are four categories of expenses—direct sales commissions, management fees, marketing costs, and overhead expenses.

Mutual funds come in two types: load and no-load. **Load funds** carry an up-front sales charge of 4% to 8.5% of the amount invested for "Class A" shares and are bought from a stockbroker, commission-based financial planner, and others who earn their living on sales commissions. A mutual fund is considered **low-load** if it carries a smaller up-front sales charge of 1% to 3%. Some funds charge a back-end load, also known as a **contingent deferred sales charge** (CDSC). You don't pay a sales fee to get into the fund, but you will incur a sales charge on the way out if you sell early. These funds, commonly called "Class B" shares, were created to combat the negative image of up-front loads. Typically, the charge declines 1% each year until it disappears after the fifth or sixth year. However, management and marketing fees are usually higher on this version of a load fund. Try to avoid this arrangement if you don't know how long you will hold the fund.

No-load funds, on the other hand, require no upfront fees to purchase shares and usually have no marketing fees. Investors deal directly with the fund company, a mutual fund supermarket (e.g., Charles Schwab, Waterhouse), or a fee-only financial planner, rather than with a broker. Some load and no-load funds also impose redemption fees to discourage investors from moving in and out of certain funds too frequently.

Both no-load and load funds charge annual money management and administrative fees. These costs are a percentage of the assets in the portfolio. These costs, in addition to the marketing/advertising fees, called a 12b-1 fee, make up a fund's **expense ratio.** The 12b-1 fee pays for advertising and distribution costs, as well as broker compensation. Deducted from shareholder assets, 12b-1 fees can range from 0.1 to 1.00%, and every shareholder pays a prorated share. Typical expense ratios, which can include a 12b-1 fee, range from 0.5% to 2% of fund portfolio assets. Beware of funds with expense ratios greater than 1.4% for stock funds, 1% for bond funds, and 0.5% for money market funds.

Generally, no-load funds have lower fees than load funds, resulting in lower expense ratios. However, there is an exception—"Class C" shares—another version sold by a broker that has no sales charge but has a higher 12b-1 and management fee than either Class A or B shares. All things being equal, low-cost funds will net you higher returns than high-cost funds. Costs matter!

Putting It All Together:
How to Find the Right Mutual Fund

Now that you are familiar with the various types of mutual funds, here are some specific guidelines for picking them.

Step 1. Identify the types of funds you need (e.g., growth) to reach your goals.

Getting started will be easier if you first focus your search on a specific type of fund with a specific investing objective. Eventually, your goal should be to build a portfolio that includes both stock and bond funds with various investment objectives and investment styles for maximum diversity. This portfolio allocation process involves assigning appropriate percentages of your total investment portfolio, no matter the size, to interest-earning (income) and stock (growth) investments. You can purchase them gradually, perhaps starting out with a balanced fund, an asset allocation fund, a lifestyle fund, or a broad-based index fund such as a "total stock market" fund. The latter tracks 7,000+ large, medium, and small U.S. companies and is offered by fund families like T. Rowe Price, Vanguard, Fidelity, Charles Schwab, and others.

Step 2. Do more reading.

Visit the library or buy some specialized books on mutual fund investing that will build on what you have learned from this unit. Some useful references are: *Mutual Funds* magazine; *Mutual Funds For Dummies* by Eric Tyson (IDG Books, 1995); *Guide to Successful No-load Fund Investing* by Sheldon Jacob (Irwin, 1995); and *The Right Way to Invest in Mutual Funds* by Walter Updegrave (Warner Books, 1996). More advanced books are John Bogle's *Bogle on Mutual Funds* (Irwin, 1994) and *Common Sense on Mutual Funds: New Imperatives for the Intelligent Investor* (John Wiley and Sons, Inc., 2000).

Step 3. Do some research on specific funds.

There are excellent tools to help with the process of narrowing the list. Personal finance magazines publish their "best buy" lists generally twice a year in February and August (e.g., *Money*, *Kiplinger's Personal Finance Magazine*, *Business Week*, and *Forbes*). *Barron's* and *The Wall Street Journal* publish a quarterly *Mutual Fund Review* that reports on all funds' categories and objectives, current and past performances, as well as fee structures. Also, the Investment Company Institute (<www.ici.org>) has excellent free publications on mutual funds.

Once you spot several funds that have consistently performed well and are aligned with your goals, go to your library's reference section to complete your research.

Rating services such as *Morningstar* and *Value Line Mutual Fund Survey* provide current data on mutual funds with a one-page report on each. This makes it easy to review and compare funds you are considering. Look at three-, five-, and ten-year periods. Last year's high flyer could be this year's dud. In addition, check out these worthwhile Web sites: <www.morningstar.com>, <www.quicken.com/investments/mutualfunds>, <www.brill.com>, and *Mutual Fund Magazine Online* at <www.mutual-funds.com>. Some sites charge a fee for online fund reports.

Step 4. Determine your selection criteria and eliminate funds.

You can whittle down the 12,000+ fund universe to a manageable list in short order by using a few criteria to help with the elimination process. For example, suppose you are looking for a stock fund to invest for retirement. Right there, you have cut the number to a little over 5,000 funds by eliminating all the bond and money market funds. Perhaps you will toss out all funds that have a sales commission, all stock funds with an expense ratio over 1.4%, funds that have an investment minimum over $3,000, any fund where the manager's tenure is less than five years, and all funds that have not outperformed 60% of comparable funds over the last three and five five years, etc. Applying these criteria as you research your favorites, pay most attention to performance, cost to invest, and risk.

Step 5. Call or write for a prospectus.

A prospectus for a mutual fund is the selling document legally required to be distributed to mutual fund investors. It describes the fund's investment strategy as well as the risks and costs of an investment.

Step 6. Make your purchase.

While you can always do business by mail, and in some cases, at a local investment center, most mutual fund groups offer a toll-free number for telephone assistance. Of course, if you are buying a fund with a sales commission, the broker or financial planner executes your order.

Step 7. Continually buy more shares.

One of the best ways to grow your investments is to use a dollar-cost averaging strategy—investing a fixed number of dollars (e.g., $50) in a mutual fund(s) at periodic intervals, usually monthly or quarterly (see Unit 8). When the price of the fund is low, your dollars buy more shares. When the fund's NAV moves higher, you will buy fewer shares. Although dollar-cost averaging does not guarantee you a profit, in most cases your average cost per share will be less than the current price.

Summary

Successful mutual fund investing requires a plan and the discipline to stick to your plan. Mutual funds are a proven winner and one of the best ways for the small investor to build wealth while managing risk. This unit has reviewed what mutual funds are and how they work, their advantages and disadvantages, fund categories and investing objectives, and, finally, the mutual fund selection process. You have what you need to get going. As the NIKE advertising slogan says, "Just do it." Start with the action steps.

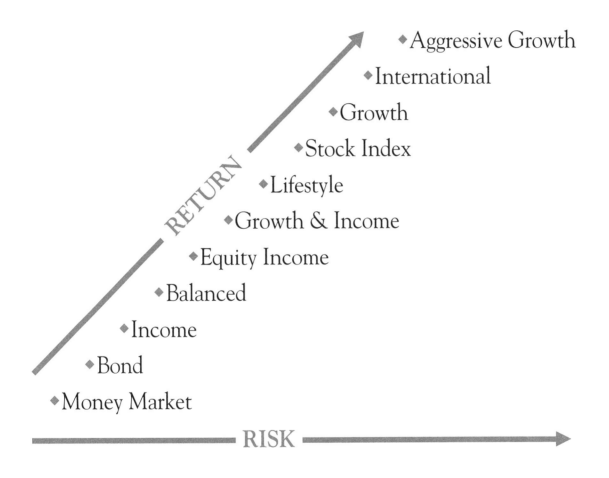

Figure 1. Risk and Return.
Adapted from AAII Mutual Funds Video Course Workbook *(1990)*.

Action Steps

✔ Take action now.
Mutual Fund Investing

Check off the steps after you have completed them.

- ❑ Make a list of long- and short-term financial goals so you can match them with an appropriate mutual fund.

- ❑ Learn about mutual fund investment choices (e.g., stock funds) available through your employer's retirement plan [e.g., 401(k), 403(b)].

- ❑ Attend an investment seminar sponsored by Cooperative Extension or financial services firms.

- ❑ Call Cooperative Extension for additional personal finance information/fact sheets, etc.

- ❑ Decide on your selection criteria (e.g., minimum deposit, low expense ratio).

- ❑ Identify specific mutual funds that match your investment goals.

- ❑ Call at least three mutual fund organizations for a prospectus.

- ❑ Do further reading on these mutual funds and mutual funds in general (e.g., prospectus, annual report, books).

- ❑ Do follow-up research using *Morningstar* or *Value Line* and compare at least three mutual funds of the same type for performance, cost, and risk.

- ❑ Complete a mutual fund application and make an investment.

- ❑ Track the progress of your fund(s) at least quarterly.

References

American Association of Individual Investors (1990). *Mutual funds video course workbook.*

Bogle, J. (1994). *Bogle on mutual funds.* New York: Irwin Professional Publishing.

Clements, J. (1998, April 4). Your starting point for mutual funds? Here are 65 of them in the annual List. *The Wall Street Journal*, C1.

Clements, J. (1994, December 10). If you're still hiding in mutual funds, maybe it's time for mutual funds. *The Wall Street Journal*, C1.

The feeling is mutual (1993, April–May). *Modern maturity*, 55–59.

Gould, E. (1992). *The New York Times guide to mutual funds.* New York: Times Books.

Newman, R. (1997, September 21). Buying bond mutual funds. *The Record*, B4.

Quinn, J. B. (1997). *Making the most of your money.* New York: Simon and Schuster.

Rowland, M. (1998). *The new common sense guide to mutual funds.* Princeton: Bloomberg Press.

Schultz, E. (1996, February 21). Bewildering class structure is lurking in the shadows of mutual fund investing. *The Wall Street Journal*, C1.

Tyson, E. (1995). *Mutual funds for dummies.* Foster City, CA: IDG Books.

Updegrave, W. (1996). *The right way to invest in mutual funds.* New York: Warner Books.

Wall Street Journal (1997). *Guide to understanding personal finance.* New York: Lightbulb Press, Inc.

Author Profile

Patricia Brennan, M.A., a Certified Financial Planner (CFP), has been a family and consumer sciences educator with Rutgers Cooperative Extension of Morris County since 1981. She is a tenured associate professor at Cook College, Rutgers University. Mrs. Brennan is also an Accredited Financial Counselor (AFC) and a Certified Housing Counselor (CHC). Pat teaches over 80 personal finance and housing classes annually. Her areas of expertise include long-term investing, asset allocation, life-cycle financial planning, and selecting mutual funds. As part of her Cooperative Extension responsibilities, she records a weekly three-minute morning radio program on station WMTR as well as daily radio spots on "Consumer Concerns" on WGHT, Pompton Lakes. She also writes for Morris County newspapers, appears regularly on Cablevision's cable TV show "Money Counts," and has made guest appearances on CNBC's "The Money Club" and News 12 New Jersey. She earned a B.S. degree in home economics from Immaculata College and her M.A. in teaching from Montclair State University.

Tax-Deferred INVESTING

Constance Y. Kratzer, Ph.D., New Mexico Cooperative Extension

This unit discusses different plans for investing money and deferring the taxes on investment earnings until a later date. Tax reduction is not the primary criterion for choosing investments, but it certainly is an important one. Tax-exempt or tax-deferred refers to the tax status of the earnings on an investment. Although these terms sound similar, they are quite different. Understanding how taxes affect different investments will help you to choose the investments that are best for you.

If no taxes are owed on money you earn from an investment, it is in the **tax-exempt** category (a.k.a., tax-free). An example of a tax-exempt investment is municipal bonds. The interest only (not any capital gains) from these investments is free of federal taxes, as well as state and local taxes, if the investor lives in the state that issued the bond. For other examples of tax-exempt securities, refer to Unit 5.

With a **tax-deferred** investment, taxes are not owed on the investment until it is sold; i.e., taxes are deferred until that time. This unit focuses on the plans available for investing on a tax-deferred basis. Upon completion of this lesson, you will be better able to recognize the benefits and drawbacks of tax-deferred investments. You also will be knowledgeable about various options for tax-deferred investments. After determining which plan is right for you, you will need to select investment product(s) to be included in the plan. Units 4, 5, and 6 provide information about the characteristics of various investment products, such as **stocks**, **bonds**, and **mutual funds**.

One of the best ways to save for retirement is through tax-deferred investments. Contributions (money added to an investment plan) to employer retirement plans and some IRAs can be made with pretax dollars (i.e., income you don't have to pay tax on), allowing you to defer taxes until you start making withdrawals. Tax-deferred investing allows you to keep money that would have been paid in taxes at the time you earned the money, leaving a greater amount available for investing.

Common Advantages of Retirement Accounts

A major advantage of tax-deferred investing is making contributions to a retirement account with pretax dollars. In many instances [e.g., 401(k) plans], the government allows taxable income to be reduced by the amount of the contribution to a tax-deferred retirement plan. As a result, you can have the same amount

TAX DEFERRAL
Postponing taxes due on an amount invested and/or its earnings until they are withdrawn from the investment, usually at retirement

STOCKS
Securities that represent a unit of ownership in a corporation

BOND
A debt instrument or IOU issued by corporations or units of government

MUTUAL FUND
An investment company that pools money from shareholders and invests in a variety of securities, including stocks, bonds, and money market securities

of money in your pocket and invest what you would have paid the government. For instance, if you are in the 27% marginal income tax bracket (decreasing to 26% in 2004–2005 and 25% in 2006) and you contribute $1,000 to a tax-deferred retirement plan, you would lower your federal income taxes by $270 (0.27 times $1,000). The savings is based on your **marginal tax rate**, i.e., the rate you pay on the highest dollar of earnings.

There are six different marginal tax rates in 2002–2003—10, 15, 27, 30, 35, and 38.6%—which will change in the future. The higher your marginal tax rate, the more you as an investor benefit from pretax dollar contributions and tax-deferred earnings. Figure 1 shows the 2002 tax rate schedules for your reference in determining marginal tax rates. These figures are adjusted annually for inflation. Between 2004 and 2006, these tax rates will be reduced as follows: 2004–2005 — 10, 15, 26, 29, 34, and 37.6%; and 2006 and after — 10, 15, 25, 28, 33, and 35%.

Single—Schedule X

If line 5 is: Over-	But not over-	The tax is:		Of the amount over-
$0	$6,000	——	10%	$0
6,000	27,950	$600.00	+15%	6,000
27,950	67,700	3,892.50	+27%	27,950
67,700	141,250	14,625.00	+30%	67,700
141,250	307,050	36,690.00	+35%	141,250
307,050	——	94,720.00	+38.6%	307,050

Head of household—Schedule Z

If line 5 is: Over-	But not over-	The tax is:		Of the amount over-
$0	$10,000	——	10%	$0
10,000	37,450	$1,000.00	+15%	10,000
37,450	96,700	5,117.50	+27%	37,450
96,700	156,600	21,115.00	+30%	96,700
156,600	307,050	39,085.00	+35%	156,600
307,050	——	91,742.50	+38.6%	307,050

Married filing jointly or Qualifying widow(er)— Schedule Y-1

If line 5 is: Over-	But not over-	The tax is:		Of the amount over-
$0	$12,000	——	10%	$0
12,000	46,700	$1,200.00	+15%	12,000
46,700	112,850	6,405.00	+27%	46,700
112,850	171,950	24,265.50	+30%	112,850
171,950	307,050	41,995.50	+35%	171,950
307,050	——	89,280.50	+38.6%	307,050

Married filing separately— Schedule Y-2

If line 5 is: Over-	But not over-	The tax is:		Of the amount over-
$0	$6,000	——	10%	$0
6,000	23,350	$600.00	+15%	6,000
23,350	56,425	3,202.50	+27%	23,350
56,425	85,975	12,132.75	+30%	56,425
85,975	153,525	20,997.75	+35%	85,975
153,525	——	44,640.25	+38.6%	153,525

Figure 1. 2002 Tax Rate Schedules.
Source: IRS Form 1040-ES (2002)

A second advantage of tax-deferred investing is that earnings grow faster because they aren't taxed until withdrawn. Instead of paying tax on the interest earned, it continues to compound until the investment is sold. Over time, the gap between the value of a taxable and a tax-deferred account, earning the same rate of interest, increases sharply. See figure 2 for an example.

Investing For Your Future

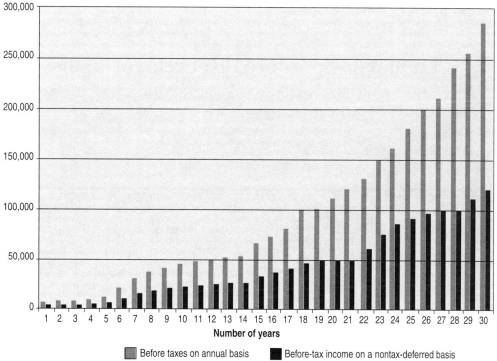

Figure 2. Comparison of a Tax-Deferred Retirement Investment with a Nontax-Deferred Investment. This figure assumes an investment of $2,000 of before-tax income on an annual basis in a retirement account where those contributions are fully tax-deductible versus investing $2,000 of before-tax income on a nontax-deferred basis. A 9% annual return is assumed on both investments, with the investment earnings in the tax-deferred account not being reduced by taxes, and the earnings in the other account being taxed annually. A marginal tax rate of 31% also is assumed. Source: Keown, A.J. (2000) *Personal finance: Turning money into wealth.* 2nd edition. Upper Saddle River, New Jersey: Prentice-Hall.

Penalties for Early Withdrawal

All tax-deferred accounts carry a penalty for withdrawing the money before age 59½. However, some types of accounts have exceptions, such as money withdrawn to be used to buy a first home, or if the owner of the account becomes disabled or dies. In addition, for some accounts, the penalty may not apply if the individual is taking equal periodic payments over his or her life expectancy for at least five years or until age 59½, whichever comes later, or for college expenses, and certain medical expenses. The penalty is usually 10% of the amount withdrawn and then, of course, federal and state income taxes also have to be paid on the withdrawal.

Types of Retirement Plans

The government allows several different types of tax-deferred retirement programs. Among these are employer-sponsored plans, plans for self-employed persons, and individual retirement accounts (IRAs). Many of the plans are named for sections of the tax code that establish these plans [e.g., 401(k) and 403(b)]. These plans differ in who is eligible to participate, administrative responsibilities, allowable contribu-

Notes

tion limits, the types of investments available in the plan, and tax consequences and penalties for early withdrawal (a 10% penalty, plus ordinary income tax, is charged for withdrawals made prior to age 59½; certain exceptions apply).

Employer-Sponsored Retirement Plans

Salary-reduction plans allow employees to deposit, through payroll deduction, part of their salary into a retirement account. There are a number of ways you, as an employee, can invest on a tax-deferred basis so that your investment will grow free of taxes and will not be taxed until you start making withdrawals. Types of employer-sponsored retirement plans include:

> **401(k)**—A retirement plan for employees, generally in private corporations, that defers the taxes on employee contributions and earnings on these contributions until retirement withdrawals are made. You can contribute up to 20% of your earnings up to a set maximum. The 2002 limit on the amount that can be contributed from income before taxes is $11,000. Contributions are deducted directly from your paycheck (e.g., 5% of your salary). Some employers contribute a match or a percentage of your contribution. Many companies also allow their employees to borrow up to one-half of the funds from their 401(k) plan for any reason. Interest paid by the employee on the money that is borrowed from his 401(k) is paid into the employee's own account.

> **403(b)**—A tax-deferred retirement plan that is similar to corporate 401(k) plans. A big difference is fewer employers match contributions, because participants are often public (read: taxpayer-funded) employees. 403(b) plans are available to employees of schools and nonprofit organizations. The 2002 limit for contributions is $11,000. The mix of available investment choices differs among institutions. Many allow participants to borrow from their account and have a catch-up provision if you have not contributed fully in the past.

> **Section 457**—This plan is similar to the 401(k) and 403(b) but is for state and local government employees. With Section 457 plans, employer matching is virtually nonexistent. The 2002 limit that you can contribute is $11,000.

Contribution limits to all of the above employer plans will be increasing in future years as follows: 2003—$12,000; 2004—$13,000; 2005—$14,000; and 2006—$15,000. In addition, starting in 2002, persons age 50 and older can make additional catch-up contributions as follows: 2002—$1,000; 2003—$2,000; 2004—$3,000; 2005—$4,000; and 2006—$5,000. Amounts will be adjusted for inflation in 2007 and after.

401(K) PLAN
A retirement savings plan, generally found in private corporations, that allows an employee to contribute pretax dollars to a company investment vehicle until the employee retires or leaves the company.

403(B) PLAN
Similar to a 401(k), a retirement savings plan for employees of a tax-exempt education or research organization or public school. Pretax dollars are contributed to an investment pool until the employee retires or terminates employment.

Self-Employed or
Small Business Retirement Plans

There also are tax-deferred plans available to individuals who are self-employed or employees of small businesses. These include:

> ✦ Keogh Plan
>
> ✦ Simplified Employee Pension Plan (SEP)
>
> ✦ Savings Incentive Match Plan for Employees (SIMPLE)

The following descriptions can help determine which plan could work for you.

Keogh Plan

Named after U.S. representative Eugene James Keogh, who first introduced the idea in 1962, this plan is available to anyone who has self-employed income. This is generally income from any unincorporated business that you conduct, whether it is your primary job or a business "on the side." Self-employed persons may contribute as much as 100% of their net self-employment income, up to a maximum amount of $40,000 per year in 2002, with periodic adjustments for inflation. For purposes of a Keogh, the definition of earned income is net profit (i.e., net income after subtracting business expenses). The money contributed to a Keogh plan is not taxed and grows in value until it is withdrawn. You may have both a Keogh plan and an IRA. If you work for an employer and are self-employed on the side, you may pay into a Keogh and also belong to the employer's retirement plans. In addition, if you have employees, you can enroll others who work for you.

To set up a Keogh plan, you must first select a bank, mutual fund, or other financial institution. Usually they will supply the needed paperwork and provide you with a prototype plan. You will be asked to choose a defined-contribution and/or a defined-benefit Keogh plan. These two options are not mutually exclusive—your plan can include both. There are three forms of defined-contribution Keogh plans:

1. A money-purchase Keogh requires you to choose a fixed percentage of your earnings and contribute that percentage every year to the plan.
2. A profit-sharing Keogh allows you to contribute a fixed percentage of business profits. You can contribute the full amount one year and less or nothing the next, depending on how the business does.
3. A combination of money-purchase and profit-sharing offers the option of contributing 100% of net income up to $40,000, but doesn't lock a business owner into high payments.

KEOGH PLAN
A qualified retirement plan for self-employed individuals and their employees to which tax-deductible contributions up to a specified yearly limit can be made if the plan meets certain requirements of the Internal Revenue Code.

SIMPLIFIED EMPLOYEE PENSION PLAN
A tax-sheltered retirement plan aimed at small businesses or at the self-employed that requires minimal paperwork to establish and maintain.

SIMPLE PLAN or SAVINGS INCENTIVE MATCH PLAN FOR EMPLOYEES
A tax-sheltered retirement plan aimed at small businesses or the self-employed that provides for some matching funds by the employer to be deposited in an employee's retirement account.

Notes

Under a defined benefit Keogh plan, rather than contribute a percentage of your earnings, you are allowed to contribute more than the annual limit imposed on defined-contribution plans. Also, the amount contributed each year can vary greatly. These plans can be complicated and costly to set up and administer because a professional actuary is required to oversee the plan. Generally, defined-benefit Keogh plans are used as a catch-up strategy by older business owners who have put off setting up a retirement plan.

SEP (Simplified Employee Pension)

Simplified Employee Pensions (SEPs) allow business owners to make contributions to their own individual retirement account (IRA) and the IRAs of their employees. Certain dollar limits and percentages of pay apply. The contribution limits are set at 15% of earned income for the employee and 13.04% for the employer. Employers must contribute the same percentage to their employees' IRA as they do to their own. One advantage to the employer or self-employed person is that contributions do not have to be made every year. Little paper work is required, it is much simpler than setting up a Keogh plan, and it does not have the reporting requirements of a Keogh. A disadvantage is that you cannot contribute as much to a SEP as you can to a Keogh plan. Generally, contributions are made by the employer and are tax-deductible to the employer.

SIMPLE Plans

A SIMPLE plan is a tax-deferred savings plan that can be set up by business owners that employ 100 or fewer employees to cover all employees and themselves. As of 1997, small employers can establish SIMPLE-IRAs or SIMPLE 401(k)s. To be covered, employees must earn at least $5,000 a year. The maximum contribution is $7,000 in 2002. In future years, contribution limits for SIMPLE plans will increase as follows: 2003—$8,000; 2004—$9,000; 2005—$10,000. In 2006 and later, the contribution limit will be adjusted for inflation. The employee's contribution reduces taxable income, and the employer's contribution reduces the business's taxable income. A SIMPLE-IRA is owned by the employee and belongs to the employee, even if employment is terminated. Like SEPs, SIMPLE-IRAs have low administrative responsibilities and costs compared to Keogh plans.

Individual Retirement Accounts (IRAs)

For individuals who qualify, another smart way to build a retirement nest egg is to take advantage of the tax-deferred growth offered by an Individual Retirement Account (IRA). An IRA is a personal retirement savings plan, which may be set up with banks, mutual fund companies, brokerage firms, or similar investment organizations. Three types of IRAs are described below.

IRA or INDIVIDUAL RETIREMENT ACCOUNT
A retirement savings plan that allows individuals to save for retirement on a tax-deferred basis. The amount of savings that is tax deductible varies according to an individual's access to pension coverage, income tax filing status, household income, and the type of IRA that is selected.

Traditional IRAs

For tax-deferment purposes, an IRA can be funded until April 15 of the following year (e.g., April 15, 2003, for the 2002 tax year). Of course, the earlier in the year an IRA is funded, the quicker that interest will begin to accumulate.

For tax years through 2001, the maximum that could be contributed in any one year was 100% of earned income up to $2,000. Your spouse could also make a $2,000 contribution. However, you don't have to make the entire contribution all at once. You can start with whatever money is available (e.g., $500) that meets the minimum amount set by the financial institutions. The 2001 tax law increased the maximum IRA limits to $3,000 for 2002–2004; $4,000 for 2005–2007; and $5,000 for 2008 and after. In addition, people age 50 and over in 2002 can contribute an additional $500 catch-up amount from 2002–2005 and an additional $1,000 for 2006 and after. Contributions can be made as long as you are under age 70½.

> Traditional IRAs may be:
>
> Tax-deductible (for taxpayers who are not participants in an employer retirement plan or plan participants with income below certain levels)
>
> Nondeductible (for taxpayers with earned income who fail to qualify for a deductible IRA)

Deductible IRAs provide a double tax benefit: contributions—and all earnings— are tax-deferred until retirement. You can also deduct (from taxable income) the full amount contributed if you are in an employer-sponsored retirement plan, but your adjusted gross income (AGI) is $34,000 or less if you are single or $54,000 or less if you are married and filing jointly (2002 amounts). Once you reach this level, a phase-out range begins. The deduction is eliminated at a maximum AGI of $44,000 for single filers and $64,000 for married joint filers (2002 amounts). Figure 3 below shows the increase in income ranges for deductible IRAs over the next six years.

Year	Joint Return	Single, Head of Household
2002	$54,000–$64,000	$34,000–44,000
2003	$60,000–$70,000	$40,000–50,000
2004	$65,000–$75,000	$45,000–55,000
2005	$70,000–$80,000	$50,000–60,000
2006	$75,000–$85,000	$50,000–60,000
2007*	$80,000–$100,000	$50,000–60,000

*And later years

Figure 3. Phase-out ranges for deductible IRAs.

The IRS no longer considers one spouse an "active participant" in a retirement plan simply because the other spouse has an employer-sponsored retirement plan. As a result, the spouse who does not have an employer-sponsored retirement plan can make a tax-deductible contribution to an IRA, provided the couple's AGI is less than $160,000.

Notes

If you withdraw money from an IRA before age 59½, there will be a 10% penalty on the amount withdrawn, and federal and state income taxes will be due on the amount withdrawn on that year's income tax return. You can withdraw funds from an IRA without a penalty after you reach age 59½. Withdrawals from a traditional IRA are taxable and are treated as ordinary income. Withdrawals must begin no later than April 1 of the year after you turn 70½.

Penalty-free withdrawals of up to $10,000 can be made from any IRA for first-time homebuyers who meet certain qualifications. Withdrawals also can be made for qualified higher education expenses incurred on behalf of the taxpayer, the taxpayer's spouse, or any of their children or grandchildren. These education withdrawal provisions include expenses related to undergraduate or graduate-level college courses.

Roth IRAs

Although contributions to a Roth IRA are not tax-deductible, qualified withdrawals are tax-exempt if made more than five years after the Roth IRA was established and the taxpayer has reached age 59½, becomes disabled, or dies. Roth IRAs accumulate like whole life insurance—they go in after-tax, accumulate tax-deferred, and come out tax-free. Another big plus: Unlike traditional IRAs, investors in a Roth IRA are not subject to the minimum distribution rules, and you can make contributions after age 70½ as a worker or spouse of a worker. Early withdrawals from a Roth IRA are tax-free and penalty-free if they satisfy the five-year holding requirement or the money is used to cover qualified first-time homebuyer expenses of up to $10,000, or if the taxpayer becomes disabled before age 59½ or dies.

Individuals can contribute up to $3,000 per year in 2002–2004 ($4,000 in 2005–2007; and $5,000 in 2008, to be adjusted for inflation in $500 increments) to a Roth IRA if they have an AGI of up to $95,000 (for married taxpayers filing a joint return, the AGI limit is $150,000). Eligibility for contributing to a Roth IRA begins to phase out for individuals with an AGI over $95,000 and ends once an individual's AGI exceeds $110,000. For joint filers, the phase-out figures are between $150,000 and $160,000. Investors can roll funds over from a traditional IRA to a Roth IRA, provided the taxpayer's AGI is $100,000 or less and he or she is not a married individual filing separately. Taxes must be paid on the amount of the conversion, in the year that the conversion is made. To determine if converting from a traditional IRA to a Roth IRA will result in a decrease in taxes, check one of the IRA calculator links on the Web site <www.rothira.com>.

Coverdell Education Savings Accounts (Formerly Known as Education IRAs)

The Coverdell Education Savings Account (ESA)—formerly known as the Education IRA—allows parents, grandparents, and others to help fund the qualified higher education expenses of a named beneficiary who is under age 18. Tax law changes made in 2001 have made this a more attractive savings vehicle for college than it was previously.

Annual contributions to Coverdell ESAs are nondeductible. The maximum contribution is $2,000 per child starting in 2002. Also, starting in 2002, the definition of qualified educational expenses expands to include elementary and secondary schools, and contributions will be allowed after a child reaches age 18. Coverdell ESA earnings can be withdrawn tax-free if used solely for the beneficiary's qualified education expenses. Any earnings not used for qualified education expenses are included in the gross income of the beneficiary in the year distributed and are subject to an additional 10% penalty tax.

The good news for parents with more than one child is that a tax-free and penalty-free rollover of account balances can be made to a Coverdell ESA to benefit a younger member of the beneficiary's family. Like the Roth IRA, eligibility for contributions to a Coverdell ESA phases out at an AGI of $95,000 to $110,000 for single tax filers. The phaseout range for married joint filers was increased to $190,000 to $220,000 for ESAs beginning in 2002.

Annuities

An annuity is a contract between the investor and a life insurance company. All annuities have two things in common:

> 1. There is no tax deduction for the money used to purchase the annuity [exception: tax-sheltered annuities in 403(b) plans].
> 2. Inside the annuity, the money compounds tax-deferred. Beyond this, each annuity has its own cost structure, characteristics, and rate of return. Taxes are paid on the earnings when money is withdrawn at retirement, either in a lump sum or as a series of periodic payments.

Annuities are sold by bankers, stockbrokers, financial planners, insurance agents, or through mutual funds, but regardless of who makes the sale, an insurance company always backs the annuity. If the annuity holder (investor) dies during the so-called accumulation phase—that is, before receiving any payments from the annuity—the beneficiary is guaranteed to receive the amount of the original investment.

Investors purchase an annuity by paying a lump sum of money (minimum purchase range from $2,000 to $10,000) or by making deposits over time. An annuity may be either an immediate annuity or a deferred annuity.

Immediate Annuities

An immediate annuity pays a lifetime income starting now. In return for a lump sum of money, the purchase of an annuity guarantees a fixed stream of income. To determine where to buy the right annuity, check the *Annuity & Life Insurance Shopper* or *Best's Retirement Income Guide* for the companies that pay the five highest monthly incomes per $1,000 invested. Go with a quality company (one that has paid consistently above average returns) that pays the most. To spread your risk, you may want to buy annuities from two or more companies or buy annuities in subsequent years.

> **ANNUITY**
> A contract by which an insurance company agrees to make regular payments to someone for life or for a fixed period in exchange for a lump sum or periodic deposits.

Deferred Annuities

Deferred annuities may be purchased in one of two ways. Single premium annuities are purchased with a lump sum, and flexible payment annuities may be purchased by installment payments over a period of years. Deferred annuities accumulate money for the future and come in two types. A **fixed annuity** pays a specified interest rate for a period of time. A **variable annuity** puts your money in stock, bond, or money market mutual funds, and returns are dependent on the financial market volatility and performance. One way to differentiate between immediate and deferred annuities is that an immediate annuity is used to distribute money, while a deferred annuity is used to accumulate money.

Payout Options

The payout from annuities may be taken in several ways. Taxes are owed when the money comes out, and there is a 10% penalty on earnings withdrawn before age 59½. You can take monthly payments for the rest of your life, or you can make periodic withdrawals. If you make regular withdrawals, part of each withdrawal is treated as taxable income, and the rest is a nontaxable return of your own capital. If you make occasional withdrawals, the entire withdrawal is treated as taxable income. Taxes are levied until you have taken all of the earnings on the original capital invested. Other payment options include taking the money in a lump sum or rolling your savings into another annuity tax-free.

When you buy an annuity, you are making a long-term commitment (15–20 years). Moving the money to another annuity may be difficult, and quitting is expensive. You usually have to pay a surrender fee to the insurance company for selling an annuity too soon (e.g., withdrawing money from an annuity after the third year). A common fee is 7% the first year which is reduced to 0% by the seventh year. Because annuities are purchased with after-tax dollars, it is usually recommended that pretax investment plans [e.g., IRAs, 401(k)s] be funded to the maximum first.

Summary

This unit has discussed the advantages of tax-deferred plans to invest for retirement. These include employer-provided plans, small business employer/employee plans, plans for the self-employed, Individual Retirement Accounts, and annuities. Tax advantages are that earnings are not taxed until funds are withdrawn, and contributions are often made with pretax dollars that are not subject to income tax. As contributions to some IRAs and annuities may not be with pretax dollars, putting the maximum in tax-deferred employer plans first will bring greater returns at retirement.

Keep in mind that there are penalties for early withdrawal on many of the plans, so those dollars that are needed before age 59½ are better invested in other accounts. Also, once you have determined which plan works for you, you still have to decide on what investments you will put in the plan. Other units in this course will help you make those decisions. Start now with the action steps. The sooner you start, the more time your money will have to grow!

Action Steps

✔ Take action now.
Tax-Deferred Investing

Check off the steps after you have completed them.

❑ Ask if your employer has a tax-deferred retirement plan [e.g., 401(k)].

❑ Find out what investment choices are available in the employer plan.

❑ Find out if your employer matches your investment dollars and, if so, by how much.

❑ Set a date to start contributing or to increase your contribution—either a dollar amount or a percentage of your salary.

❑ If you are self-employed, determine the type of retirement fund you could start, set an amount, and begin making contributions.

❑ Investigate IRAs and determine which type is best for your age and income level.

❑ Increase contributions to your tax-deferred plan each time your pay increases.

A "sunset" provision was placed in the 2001 tax law to eliminate all of the tax law changes, such as higher contribution limits and catch-up amounts for tax-deferred retirement accounts, on December 31, 2010. If these changes are not made permanent by a future Congress, the contribution limits will revert to 2001 levels in 2011, and the catch-up provisions will be eliminated.

References

2001 tax law summary (2001). Albany, NY: Newkirk Press.

Brennan, P. Q. *The ins and outs of IRAs*. Rutgers Cooperative Extension curriculum.

Garman, E. T. & Forgue, R. E. (2000). *Personal finance*, 6th Edition. Boston: Houghton Mifflin Company.

Goodman, J. E. (1997). *Everyone's money book*. Chicago: Dearborn Financial Publishing, Inc.

Keown, A. J. (1998). *Personal finance: Turning money into wealth*. Upper Saddle River, NJ: Prentice-Hall.

O'Neill, B. (1997) *Investing in annuities: What you need to know*. Rutgers Cooperative Extension curriculum.

Pond, J. A. (1998). *Personal financial planning handbook with forms and checklists*, 2nd edition. Boston: Warham, Gorham & Lamont.

Pond, J. A. (1993). *The new century family money book*. New York: Dell Books.

Retirement Plans for Small Businesses. <www.irs.ustreas.gov/bus_info/ep/retirement.html>

SEP (Simplified Employee Pensions) <www.dol.gov/dol/pwba/public/pubs/main.htm>

SIMPLE (Savings incentive match plan for employees of small employers) <www.dol.gov/dol/pwba/public/pubs/main.htm>.

Tyson, E. (1994). *Personal finance for dummies*. San Mateo, CA: IDG Books Worldwide, Inc.

White, A. (1999). *The basics of retirement plans*. Class curriculum, Virginia Cooperative Extension.

Author Profile

Constance Y. Kratzer, Ph.D., is an extension specialist in family resource management, Home Economics Extension Department, New Mexico State University. She received her Ph.D. from Michigan State University in 1991. She provides statewide program leadership in the areas of financial management and management of time and energy. Her research has been in the areas of perception of economic well-being, planning for retirement by the self-employed, and workplace financial education. She received an Emerging Leaders Award from Michigan State University in 1996.

INVESTING WITH $mall Dollar Amount$

——— Barbara O'Neill, Ph.D., CFP, Rutgers Cooperative Extension ———

Earlier units in this course have discussed specific types of investment products (e.g., mutual funds) and various investment prerequisites. Unfortunately, and erroneously, many people think that they need a substantial sum of money to start investing. This is simply not the case. The objective of this unit is to demonstrate that investing is possible, even on a "shoestring" budget. Investing can be done with as little as $25 (e.g., a U.S. savings bond), and a variety of investments (e.g., Treasury securities, unit investment trusts, and many mutual funds) are available for an initial outlay of $1,000 or less. Once you've taken care of "the basics" (e.g., reduced household debt, purchased adequate insurance, and set aside an emergency reserve of at least three months' expenses), you are ready to explore affordable investment options. This way, your money will earn a higher rate of return over time than a certificate of deposit or passbook savings account to help you achieve important financial goals. This unit will discuss investments that can be purchased for a thousand dollars or less and are suitable for beginning investors whose largest asset is their future earning ability.

The 2001 Retirement Confidence Survey found that many American workers said it was "reasonably possible" to set aside $20 a week for retirement (47% of those not currently saving and 65% of those who are). While this may not sound like a lot of money, over time it really adds up. At a 5% annual real rate of return, an investor would have $36,100 more than they would otherwise have in 20 years ($65,500 with a 10% return), according to the Employee Benefit Research Institute. In 30 years, the figures for 5% and 10% returns are $72,600 and $188,200, respectively, and in 40 years, the figures are even more dramatic: $131,900 with a 5% return and $506,300 when $20 per week is invested to earn 10%.

Getting Started: Investing Tax-Deferred

If saving for retirement is one of your financial goals, a good place to start investing is a **tax-deferred employer retirement plan** [e.g., **401(k)s** and **403(b)s**] (see Unit 7 for more information). Many employers require only a minimum deposit amount (e.g., $10) per paycheck or a low percentage (e.g., 1% or 2%) of pay to enroll.

> Three advantages of employer savings plans are:
> ✦ A federal tax deduction for the amount contributed (e.g., if you contribute $1,000, you do not pay tax on this income)
> ✦ Tax-deferred growth of principal and investment earnings
> ✦ Automatic payroll deduction

In addition, almost 80% of 401(k) plans and about 30% of 403(b)s provide employer matching. For every dollar a worker contributes, an employer might contribute a quarter, fifty cents, or even a dollar. This is "free money" that should not be passed up.

If you're already investing in an employer plan, consider increasing the amount contributed by 1% (or more) of pay. The most painless time to do this is when you receive a promotion or raise because you're already accustomed to living on less and won't miss the extra contribution. The extra savings (e.g., 2% of pay), combined with a pay raise, should be more or less "a wash." As chef Emeril Lagasse of the Food Network would say, "Kick it up a notch!" Over time, the extra amount of savings that will accumulate is impressive, especially for younger workers and workers at higher salary levels. According to Boston-based Advantage Publications, a company that produces financial education materials including a slide rule-type chart called the *401(k) Booster Calculator* (1-800-323-6809), investing just 1% more of your pay can translate into tens of thousands of extra dollars by retirement age.

As an example, 1% of a $30,000 salary is $300 ($5.77 weekly). According to Advantage Publications, if a 35-year-old worker earning a $30,000 salary increases his/her contribution to an employer plan by 1%, he/she would have an additional $55,680 at age 65. This example assumes an 8% average annual investment return and 4% average annual pay increases. If the extra 1% increase also triggers an additional 1% match by their employer, this figure can be doubled to $111,360.

The beauty of investing in employer plans is that you are using pretax dollars. For every dollar you invest, Uncle Sam subsidizes this investment by that amount multiplied by your tax bracket. For example, if you contribute $1,000 to an employer plan and are in the 15% marginal tax bracket, your after-tax cost is only $850 [$1,000 – ($1,000 x 0.15)]. In the 27% marginal tax bracket (decreasing to 26% in 2004–2005 and 25% in 2006), the out-of-pocket cost is even less: $730 [$1,000 – ($1,000 x 0.27)]. Most employers adjust workers' withholding to reflect this tax savings, thereby freeing up more money in each paycheck to invest. In addition, taxes are deferred on investment earnings, which provides increased growth of principal over time.

If you don't have an employer plan or have "maxed out" contributions to an employer plan and are looking for another tax-deferred investment, consider an **individual retirement account (IRA)**. The good news for IRA investors with small dollar amounts is that you don't have to invest the maximum allowable contribution ($3,000 in 2002–2004; $4,000 in 2005–2007; and $5,000 in 2008 and after, to be adjusted for inflation; additional catch-up contributions are available starting in 2002 for persons age 50 and older) all at once. You simply need to meet the minimum amounts (e.g., $250 or $500) required for the investments you select (e.g., a zero-coupon bond or mutual fund).

One way to accumulate IRA money, for example, $2,000, by year-end is to open a "Holiday Club" at a local bank. Simply deposit $40 weekly in a club plan throughout the year and you'll have $2,000 ($40 x 50 weeks) for an IRA deposit when the last coupon is clipped. By 2008, you can put $5,000 a year in an IRA or $100 a week ($100 x 50 weeks). As discussed in Unit 7, there are two types of IRAs: a traditional (deductible or nondeductible) IRA and a Roth IRA. To choose the IRA that will provide the highest amount of after-tax income, consult one or more "IRA calculators" on the Web site <www.rothira.com> or check with a financial advisor.

Buying Stocks With Small Dollar Amounts

Not too long ago, to build a diversified portfolio of stocks, you may have needed $30,000 to $50,000 or more. That was the cost to purchase a round lot of 100 shares of each of ten or 12 different stocks at an average cost of $30 to $50 per share. Today, thanks to the popularity of investment clubs and the increase in both online trading and stocks that can be purchased directly from sponsoring companies, you can make a purchase for far fewer dollars. Making small stock purchases no longer has to be costly or embarrassing (e.g., asking a broker to trade a few shares), as it used to be. Direct stock investing today is easy and affordable.

As described in detail in Unit 9, **investment clubs** generally assess members from $25 to $100 monthly, which is pooled to make club stock purchases. The amount of "dues" is decided by individual clubs based on the preferences of their members. Some investment club members also choose to invest additional dollars above the required amount. As for **online trading** (also discussed in Unit 9), several of more than 100 electronic brokerage firms in existence today require $1,000 or less to open an account, although a minimum of between $2,500 and $15,000 is typical. Stocks that can be **purchased directly from participating companies** often require initial investments of $1,000 or less, with subsequent investments (called OCPs or optional cash payments) of as little as $25.

Adequate diversification in a portfolio of individual stocks can, therefore, be achieved without spending a fortune. According to the National Association of Investors Corporation (NAIC), stocks can be grouped into 12 industry sectors. Consider the following example of an investment club stock portfolio that incorporates these sectors. The initial purchase of a diversified stock portfolio costs less than $3,000.

INVESTMENT CLUBS
Organizations of investors who meet and contribute money regularly toward the purchase of securities.

5 shares @ $35 of a building/forestry stock	$175
5 shares @ $27 of a financial services company stock	$135
5 shares @ $43 of a "consumer growth" (e.g., soft drink) stock	$215
5 shares @ $51 of a "consumer staple" (e.g., food) stock	$255
5 shares @ $39 of a "consumer cyclical" (e.g., car) stock	$195
5 shares @ $62 of a technology (e.g., computer) stock	$310
5 shares @ $48 of a capital goods (e.g., machinery) stock	$240
5 shares @ $18 of an energy (e.g., oil) stock	$90
5 shares @ $56 of a materials (e.g., paper company) stock	$280
5 shares @ $73 of a transportation (e.g., air freight) stock	$365
5 shares @ $21 of a utility (e.g., electric company) stock	$105
5 shares @ $67 of a conglomerate company stock	$335

In this example, the total cost of these shares is $2,700. Add on the fees that most companies with stock purchase plans charge (e.g., enrollment fees and fees to reinvest dividends or buy and sell shares), and the cost is undoubtedly higher, maybe $3,000.

Finding quality companies with affordable minimum investment amounts can be a challenge for individual investors, as well as investment clubs. It may also take several years to develop a diversified portfolio like the one described above if minimum amounts of $500 or more are required. Fortunately, the number of companies that allow investors to purchase shares directly has increased in recent years. By 2000, over 1,600 companies offered shareholder investment plans where dividends are invested in additional shares. Of these, **dividend reinvestment plans (DRIPs)** allow investors to make direct stock purchases only after they acquire an initial share elsewhere. Almost 500 companies offer **direct-purchase plans (DPPs or "no-load stocks")** where even the first share of stock can be purchased from the sponsoring company.

In addition to their affordability, another advantage of DRIPs and DPPs is a discount on the price of shares, which can help stretch limited investment dollars. Approximately one in ten companies that sell shares directly to investors offer a 3% to 5% discount on initial purchases and/or OCPs. Of course, the quality of a company, and not a discount on its stock, should be your primary consideration. If you're picking a quality company, however, it's nice to be able to purchase stock on sale. An increasing number of DRIPs and DPPs also allow investors to set up IRAs, although an annual fee of $25 or $50 is generally charged.

DRIPs and DPPs appeal to investors who are willing to do their own research rather than consult a broker. There are several helpful references available for investors who wish to learn more about purchasing stock directly from issuing companies. Among them are the books *No-Load Stocks* and *Buying Stocks Without a Broker* by Charles B. Carlson and the Web sites <www.netstockdirect.com>, <www.dripinvestor.com>, and <www.dripcentral.com>.

Buying Fixed-Income Investments With Small Dollar Amounts

Fixed-income investments are securities that provide regular interest or dividend payments and, in many cases, a return of principal at maturity. Their primary objective is income with limited, if any, growth potential. As noted in Unit 5, the rate of return on a fixed-income investment can be fixed throughout its holding period (e.g., bonds) or can fluctuate with the general movement of interest rates (e.g., Series EE U.S. savings bonds and money market mutual funds).

Most fixed-income investments, including all marketable **U.S. Treasury securities** (see Unit 5) purchased since August 1998, require a minimum purchase of $1,000 or less. Formerly, $10,000 was required to purchase Treasury bills and $5,000 for Treasury notes with less than a five-year maturity. Treasury bills are issued with

 Investing For Your Future

maturities of three and six months and Treasury notes with maturities of two, five and ten years. All Treasury securities are backed by the "full faith and credit" of the U.S. government and can be sold prior to maturity in secondary markets. Periodic government Treasury auctions determine the interest rate earned by investors. Generally, the longer the maturity date, the higher the rate of interest a Treasury security (and all bonds) pay, because an investor's money is "tied up" (subject to interest rate fluctuations and unavailable to invest elsewhere) for a longer period of time.

Interest earned on Treasury securities is exempt from state and local income taxes. Another characteristic is that, like all bonds, Treasuries are subject to interest rate risk (when interest rates rise, bond prices decrease and vice versa). Treasury securities can be purchased from a bank or brokerage firm with a $50 to $75 fee or directly from the Federal Reserve System's "Treasury Direct" program at no charge. For additional information, contact the Bureau of the Public Debt at 202-874-4000 for the location of the nearest Federal Reserve Bank or the Web site <www.publicdebt.treas.gov>.

Corporate bonds are IOUs issued by for-profit companies and can be purchased in denominations of $1,000. (In the secondary market, corporate bonds can cost more or less than $1,000.) Like Treasury securities, investors deposit a sum of $1,000 or more and receive a fixed amount of interest at regular intervals, generally every six months. For example, an investor holding a corporate bond paying 7% interest would receive $70 in two semi-annual payments of $35. Barring any problems with company finances, bond payments continue until bonds are called or principal is returned at maturity (e.g., 30 years). Conservative investors should select "investment-grade" bonds issued by corporations rated BBB or higher by a major rating service such as Moody's or Standard and Poor's.

Another type of fixed-income investment that can be purchased with a small dollar amount is a **zero-coupon bond** (a.k.a., zeros). These are bonds issued by certain levels of government (local, state, and federal) or corporations at a deep discount to face value. Unlike other bonds that pay semi-annual interest, zero-coupon bonds don't pay out anything until maturity, at which time an investor receives the face value, generally $1,000. The table below illustrates the amount of money required initially to purchase a zero-coupon bond that will mature to $1,000 at three different yields and maturities:

Table 1. Amounts Required to Purchase a Zero-Coupon Bond With $1,000 Face Value

Years to Maturity	Yield to Maturity						
	6%	7%	8%	9%	10%	11%	12%
25	226	179	141	111	87	69	54
15	412	356	308	267	231	201	174
5	744	709	676	644	614	585	558

Note that, the longer the time horizon to maturity and the higher the investment yield, the less an investor needs to deposit up front to guarantee a return of $1,000 at a future date. Brokers often require a transaction with a $5,000 face value, however, so the amounts in the chart would need to be multiplied by five to determine the amount needed to invest initially. For example, a purchase of five 25-year zero-coupon bonds earning 8% would require an up-front deposit of $705 ($141 x 5), which would increase in value to $5,000 in 25 years. A disadvantage of zeros is that the "phantom income" (interest that increases the amount originally invested to full face value) is taxable each year, even though this interest is not received until maturity. For this reason, zeros are often recommended for tax-deferred accounts (e.g., IRAs and Keoghs or SEPs for the self-employed).

Series EE and I U.S. Savings Bonds (see Unit 5) are also well-suited to those with small dollar amounts. Series I bonds are an inflation-adjusted savings bond introduced by the Treasury Department in September 1998. Like inflation-adjusted marketable Treasury securities that were introduced in 1997, the principal amount of Series I bonds is adjusted semi-annually for inflation. Series I bonds are available at most commercial banks and many other financial institutions.

Like Treasury securities, savings bonds are a debt instrument of the U.S. government, and income earned is completely exempt from state and local taxes. They can be purchased in denominations ranging from $50 to $10,000. Series EE bonds cost one-half their face value (e.g., $25 for a $50 bond), and Series I bonds are sold at par (e.g., $50 for a $50 bond). Many employers also offer savings bond purchase programs via payroll savings, where bonds can be purchased with as little as $5 or $10 per paycheck. Another way to purchase savings bonds is the U.S. Savings Bonds EasySaver Plan, introduced in November 1998, which provides for the regular purchase of bonds by automatically debiting your checking or savings account. Small business owners can use EasySaver as a way to provide a hassle-free employee benefit. Further information on EasySaver is available by calling 1-877-811-SAVE (7283) or from the Web site <www.easysaver.gov>.

Series EE bonds earn interest based on market yields for five-year Treasury securities. The rate for EE bonds purchased since May 1997 is 90% of the average yield on five-year securities for the preceding six months. Bonds cashed in before five years are subject to a three-month penalty. For example, if an investor redeems a bond after 18 months, they will earn 15 months of interest.

Savings bond rates are announced each May and November for the following six months. Thus, the six-month earning period for rates announced on May 1 is from May through October and, for rates announced on November 1, from November through April. Series EE bonds and I bonds earn interest for 30 years that is exempt from state and local income taxes. Special tax benefits are also available for Series EE bonds and I bonds cashed in for education expenses by qualified taxpayers.

Notes

Unit Investment Trusts:
Diversification For $1,000

Unit Investment Trusts (UITs) are a low-cost diversified investment product that can include either fixed-income securities (e.g., municipal bonds, Ginnie Maes) or stock. UITs are sold to investors by brokerage firms in small denominations called units. The cost of a unit is generally $1,000. The securities that comprise a UIT are professionally selected and of a similar type (e.g., investment-grade municipal bonds with 30-year maturities). Unlike mutual funds, however, UITs are not professionally managed. Instead, the securities in the portfolio are simply held to maturity to generate interest or dividends, which are periodically distributed proportionately to investors. If a UIT includes bonds that are called (redeemed by the issuer prior to maturity), investors get back part of their principal early. When the last security in a UIT portfolio is redeemed, the trust ceases to exist.

UITs offer diversification at a low cost. For just $1,000, an investor can become part-owner of a portfolio of, perhaps, 30 municipal bonds that would sell individually for $5,000 and would require a total of $150,000 to purchase. UITs can also be used to purchase units of Ginnie Maes, which are portfolios of VA (Veterans Administration) and FHA (Federal Housing Authority) mortgage securities packaged by the Government National Mortgage Association (GNMA).

Ginnie Maes typically sell in minimum denominations of $25,000, so investing in them directly through a UIT makes them affordable for small investors. Investors in Ginnie Maes and Ginnie Mae UITs receive both interest and a return of principal as homeowners repay their mortgages. Distributions are generally paid monthly, and the interest portion is taxable.

While originally developed as a vehicle to sell fixed-income securities, UITs have also been used to sell stocks. Common UIT stock investments are trusts that buy equal shares of the ten highest yielding stocks that make up the widely quoted Dow Jones Industrial Average (DJIA) stock index (a.k.a., "The Dow Ten" or "Dogs of the Dow"). The "Dogs of the Dow" is considered a "value investing" strategy because it invests in out-of-favor stocks that offer better bargains among the 30 large company stocks that comprise the DJIA.

Like bond and Ginnie Mae trusts, "Dow Ten" UITs are packaged and sold through brokerage firms, generally in units of $1,000 each. Instead of having to spend upwards of $50,000 to buy 100 shares of the Dow 10 stocks, ownership can be achieved at a fraction of this cost. Of course, there is "no free lunch," and UITs of all types (stocks and fixed-income securities) also have their downside. The first drawback is brokerage commissions, which are generally 3% to 5% of the initial purchase. To amortize this expense over time, it generally makes sense to "buy and hold" a UIT until it is dissolved. UITs containing bonds that can be called also are subject to unpredictable distributions and reinvestment risk (the risk of having to reinvest principal at a lower interest rate).

Mutual Funds: A Shoestring Investor's Friend

Mutual funds are a professionally managed portfolio of securities such as stocks, bonds, and real estate investment trusts that are sold to investors in units called shares (see Unit 6, which deals exclusively with mutual funds). The market price of fund shares fluctuates daily in response to market conditions and the performance of securities within a fund. Unlike UITs, mutual fund portfolios are always in a state of flux as securities are bought and sold. Unless they are closed to new investors, mutual funds are constantly receiving "new money" from investors and also must meet shareholder redemptions upon request.

The amount of money required to purchase shares in a mutual fund varies considerably. Some funds require an initial investment of $250 or $500 (or less), while others require $10,000 or even $25,000 to open an account. Like banks, mutual funds are free to set their own purchase and redemption policies. Unfortunately, many mutual funds with low initial minimums also have high expense ratios (the percentage of fund assets deducted annually for management and operational expenses). Therefore, in addition to the initial investment amount, fund expenses, objectives, and historical performance also need to be considered when making a selection.

What happens if you find a great fund but it requires more money than you have available? Don't despair! In three instances, mutual funds typically reduce their entrance requirements to a more "shoestring" level. The first exception is for **retirement accounts** such as simplified employee pensions (SEPs) and IRAs. As noted previously, federal law limits the maximum annual IRA contribution. Mutual funds that require more than the contribution limit for regular accounts must, therefore, allow a lower amount in order to comply with this rule. For example, mutual funds that require $5,000 to open a taxable account may require $3,000 (2002–2003 IRA limit) or less for retirement accounts.

A second instance where initial fund purchase requirements are lowered are **Uniform Gifts/Transfers to Minors Act** (a.k.a., UGMA/UTMA or "custodial" accounts). These are accounts established for a minor child, generally for college savings. Once a child reaches the age of majority in their state (age 18 or 21), this money is theirs to do with as they please. Again, mutual funds that charge several thousand dollars to open a regular account may accept less for minors' accounts. The T. Rowe Price mutual fund family, for example, typically requires a $2,500 minimum initial investment but only $1,000 for UGMA/UTMA accounts and retirement plans.

The third way to purchase shares in an otherwise "out-of-reach" mutual fund is to open an **automatic investment plan (a.k.a., "sharebuilder" or "asset builder" account)**. Typically, this is done through direct deposit. On the application form, an investor authorizes a mutual fund to deduct a certain amount (often a minimum of $25 or $50) periodically from his/her bank account or paycheck, which is used to purchase fund shares. In addition to the convenience of not having to remember to

write a check, this strategy also avoids the temptation of spending the money first (out of sight, out of mind).

Mutual funds, recognizing that they are encouraging a long-term relationship, generally provide a price break or waive their minimum account requirements completely for automatic investment programs. For example, many Fidelity funds require $2,500 to open an account and $250 for subsequent deposits. Investors who enroll in Fidelity's "Automatic Account Builder"ˢᴹ investment plan still need $2,500 for a regular account, and $500 for retirement accounts, but only $100 for subsequent deposits, which can be made monthly or quarterly.

All-In-One Mutual Funds

What if you have money for only one fund and want to include several asset classes (e.g., stocks, bonds, cash)? Not a problem. This, too, can be done on a shoestring budget. The trick is to select a fund that invests in several asset classes and also has an affordable minimum. Three types of "hybrid" funds that combine asset classes are balanced, asset allocation, and life-cycle funds.

◆ **Balanced funds** offer a mix of stocks and bonds, typically 60% to 70% of the portfolio in blue-chip (high-quality companies that pay dividends) stocks and 30% to 40% in investment-grade corporate bonds or federal government securities.

◆ **Asset allocation funds** typically include cash, in addition to stocks and bonds, and may include both U.S. and foreign securities. The percentage of funds in each asset class is determined by the fund manager, who attempts to earn the highest return possible by switching positions according to market conditions.

◆ **Life-cycle funds** are the third type of "hybrid" mutual fund. Like asset allocation funds, they contain a mixture of stocks, bonds, and cash.

The key difference between a life-cycle fund and an asset allocation fund is that life-cycle funds also include three or four "portfolios" with varying percentages of funds in each asset class. These portfolios are designed to fit investors of various ages or risk tolerance levels. An example is the Vanguard Group's "LifeStrategy Portfolios." Investors have a choice of four asset mixes ranging from income (60% bonds, 20% stock, and 20% cash) to growth (80% stock and 20% bonds). Some life-cycle funds follow an asset allocation strategy indefinitely, while others (usually those with a future date in their title) gradually become more conservative over time as investors get older. Some mutual fund families also offer "funds of funds" that invest in a combination of funds within their family. Two examples are Vanguard STAR ($1,000 minimum) and T. Rowe Price Spectrum ($2,500 minimum; $1,000 for IRAs; no minimum for automatic investment accounts).

Another way to obtain broad diversification with limited funds is to purchase an index fund. Index funds track the performance of a market benchmark, such as the Standard & Poor's 500 stock index. With limited funds for just one "core" fund, an investor might select a "total stock market" index fund that tracks over 7,000 large, medium, and small U.S. companies. Some index funds, such as those offered by Charles Schwab and ASM, can be purchased for $1,000. With extra funds, an investor can expand into additional index fund types (e.g., bonds, international securities) or into actively managed funds within these market sectors.

Let's take a look at how a "shoestring" mutual fund portfolio might look. Let's say that you have $2,000 to invest and your asset allocation mix is 10% cash, 30% bonds, and 60% stock. Within the 60% stock portion, you want to invest half in large company stocks and half in small company stocks. Your asset allocation might be as follows: $200 in a money market mutual fund, $600 in a bond mutual fund, and $600, respectively, in large and small company stock funds. With just $1,000 to invest, you'd place $100 in the money market fund, $300 in the bond fund, and $300 in each of the two stock funds. Of course, the trick will be finding specific funds that accept small deposits, but, as noted previously, this is often possible with automatic investing programs (i.e., DRIPs and DPPs).

Once a mutual fund account is established, resolve to add to it frequently using a strategy called **dollar-cost averaging** (see Unit 2 for details). With this strategy, shares are purchased at regular intervals (e.g., monthly) with a fixed dollar amount (e.g., $100). Dollar-cost averaging takes the emotion out of investing, because share purchases are made on a regular basis regardless of what is happening in the financial markets. In addition, most investors don't have large sums to invest, but rather, small sums periodically as they earn it.

Summary

You don't need a last name like "Gates" or "Trump" to become an investor. What you do need are investments that make it easy to get started with small dollar amounts. This unit has reviewed a variety of options ranging from tax-deferred employer retirement plans and IRAs to conservative U.S. Treasury and Series EE savings bonds to growth-oriented stocks and stock index funds. There's no time like the present to become an investor. Follow the action steps and you're on your way.

Shoestring Investment Comparison Worksheet

Characteristic	Investment #1	Investment #2	Investment #3
Guaranteed or Recent Investment Rate of Return (e.g., 7%)			
Minimum Initial Deposit Amount (e.g., $500)			
Minimum Subsequent Deposit Amount (e.g., $50)			
Up-Front Cost or Commission, if any			
Investment Objective (e.g., growth, income)			

Action Steps

Take action now.

Investing with Small Dollar Amounts

Check off the steps after you have completed them.

- ☐ Increase contributions to your tax-deferred plan each time your pay increases.

- ☐ Establish and maintain a reserve emergency fund (see Unit 1 for details).

- ☐ Reduce household expenses to free up money to invest (see Unit 3 for details).

- ☐ Make a list of financial goals (e.g., retirement, college) using the "$mart Financial Goal-Setting Worksheet" in Unit 1. Match the goals with appropriate investments.

- ☐ Investigate investment options available through your employer [e.g., 401(k) and savings bond purchase plans].

- ☐ Attend an employer-sponsored investment seminar or classes sponsored by Cooperative Extension or financial services firms.

- ☐ Calculate whether a traditional or Roth IRA is best for you, based on individual factors such as household income and age.

- ☐ Identify at least three "shoestring" investments that match your goals and available cash flow.

- ☐ Research these investments and compare at least three specific products (e.g., three large company growth funds). Use the "Shoestring Investment Comparison Worksheet" to record the key features of each.

- ☐ Dollar-cost average mutual fund purchases and/or enroll in an automatic investment program.

- ☐ Investigate the initial minimum deposits required for specific investments and ways that they can be reduced (e.g., automatic investment plan).

References

2001 retirement confidence survey summary of findings (2001). Washington, DC: Employee Benefit Research Institute.

401(k) booster calculator (1997). Boston: Advantage Publications 1-800-323-6809.

Carlson, G. (1998, Sept.). Budget funds. *Mutual Funds*, 50–51.

Clements, J. (1996, December 10). Strapped for cash? Mutual-fund firms make it easy for investors to get started. *The Wall Street Journal*, C1.

Clements, J. (1995, February 28). For novice investors on small budgets, there are plenty of ways to start out. *The Wall Street Journal*, C1.

Investing: Getting started with small amounts (1998, January). *Money Matters*, 2(1), 1, 7.

LaPlante, C. (1998). *Wall street on a shoestring*. New York: Avon Books.

No-minimum funds let you start with $1 (1995, April). *Mutual Funds*, 114–115.

O'Neill, B. (1998). *Investing on a shoestring*, class curriculum, Rutgers Cooperative Extension.

O'Neill, B. (1997). *So where do I put that $2,000?* Rutgers Cooperative Extension FS #883.

Rowland, M. (1998). Building a portfolio on a shoestring budget. *Money Insider* <www.moneycentral.msn.com>.

Updegrave, W. (1996). *The right way to invest in mutual funds*. New York: Warner Books.

Yakoboski, P., Ostuw, P., & Hicks, J. (1998). *What is your savings personality? 1998 retirement confidence survey*. Washington DC: EBRI Issue Brief Number 200.

Author Profile

Barbara O'Neill, Ph.D., holds the rank of full professor in the Family & Consumer Sciences Department at Cook College, Rutgers University. She has been a family and consumer sciences educator in Sussex County, New Jersey since 1978 and is a certified financial planner (CFP), an accredited financial counselor (AFC), and a certified housing counselor. Dr. O'Neill has written over 1,500 consumer newspaper articles and over 100 articles and abstracts for professional journals and conference proceedings. Dr. O'Neill is also the author of four books, two financial case study books published by Rutgers University, and *Saving On A Shoestring* and *Investing On A Shoestring*, trade books published by Dearborn Financial Publishing.

Getting Help: Investing Resources

Linda Kirk Fox, Ph.D., University of Idaho Cooperative Extension System

This unit highlights three popular ways that individual investors can learn more about investing and get reliable investment information. The first is by joining an investment club. The second is by using a computer to go online and get information about investing from the Internet. The third is by reading various publications recommended within this unit .

Investment Clubs

Why start or join an investment club? There are basically three reasons to join an investment club—education, fun, and potential financial gain. The club hopes to do well and make profits; however, financial gains are not guaranteed. Clubs provide a social atmosphere that makes learning about investing fun. Investment clubs differ from other clubs, however, in that individuals are not merely members of the club but are "partners." Typically, there are ten to 20 partners in a club. Partnership agreement forms are filed, and guidelines are established for the club. Guidelines include how much and how often partners must pay fees to the club and how to withdraw funds paid in and profits made. Guidelines are also set for the order of business at each meeting. A typical club meeting will have an update from the treasurer, an educational program, a presentation by partners presenting stocks or investments to buy, and updates from partners who are "watching" the club's current investments.

Advantages of an Investment Club

✦ You can learn from others who have been investing longer.
✦ You are pooling money and making joint decisions.
✦ This joint effort may be very comforting if you're hesitant about making investment decisions on your own.

Clubs require "dues" in the form of a set payment. These payments, typically $25 to $100 a month, are used by the club to buy stocks, bonds, and other investments. Regular payments such as monthly dues may make it easier for you to set aside money for investments. Like paying a bill each month, you'll write a check to the club for investing. The clubs function as a learning environment with partners tak-

ing turns giving educational programs and presenting stocks or other investments to study and to consider for purchase.

Disadvantages of an Investment Club

There are also some disadvantages to investment clubs. Financial decisions must be made year-round. For that reason, investment clubs differ from many clubs in that they must meet throughout the year. The stock market closes for only a few national holidays and certainly doesn't take an extended summer vacation. These clubs require a commitment by partners to attend meetings; hold offices such as president, secretary, and treasurer; and present educational programs. Just like any group of individuals, you may not always agree. Many clubs decide what to buy and sell with a simple vote, with the majority ruling. If you join a club, be prepared to accept decisions made by the majority of the partners even if you disagree with the investment decision.

Each investment club will establish procedures for operations, such as how often to meet and where, how much dues to charge, how new partners join, the minimum time to stay in the club, and how to pay out partners who must leave the club. Clubs must also establish criteria for investments and decide how to diversify the **portfolio**. The club will decide if a portion of their club's investments will be speculative or somewhat risky in nature, conservative, or growth- or income-oriented. Clubs may also set a policy as to what portion of the investments will be in stocks, mutual funds, or bonds, as well as set criteria for buying and selling. Most clubs, however, know that regardless of general market conditions, funds will be fully invested, and not held in cash.

Investment clubs may also establish policies about what kind of industries or companies they will not include in their portfolio. For example, the club may decide not to invest in stocks of tobacco or liquor manufacturers. The club may set a policy to invest in companies that are environmentally friendly. Criteria may even include how the company treats employees or the number of women and minorities in key leadership positions.

Sources of Information for and About Investment Club Investing

Investment clubs themselves use a variety of sources to obtain information about stocks, mutual funds, and bonds. Clubs or individual members in the club may choose to subscribe to the *Value Line Investment Survey*, business periodicals, and magazines. The *Value Line Investment Survey* provides analysis of the information contained in the **annual reports** of a company. The analysis includes a look at the company's financial history, current financial health (debt), and future prospects. Public libraries often subscribe to *Value Line Investment Survey* and other resources. They also may provide access to the Internet. Investment clubs will sometimes work with a broker who provides educational information, holds funds in the in-

PORTFOLIO
The combined holdings of more than one stock, bond, commodity, real estate investment, or other asset by an individual, club, or institutional investor.

ANNUAL REPORT
Public companies are required to file an annual report with the Securities and Exchange Commission detailing the preceding year's financial results and plans for the upcoming year. The report contains financial information concerning a company's assets, liabilities, earnings, profits, and other year-end statistics.

vestment account, and buys and sells investments as decided by the club membership.

Companies file regular reports with the U.S. Securities and Exchange Commission (SEC) that are obtainable on the Internet. Companies publish annual reports in a slick, magazine-length format to give to shareholders, the media, and interested investors. Financial charts in the form of a balance sheet inform investors of assets (things of value owned by the company) and liabilities (claims against the firm, such as debt and taxes). The income statements contained in an annual report can help investors understand the profitability of the company over time.

Investment clubs may choose to have a stock selection committee. This committee, representing a few partners, will do the initial research on potential investments, follow the established club criteria or policies, and present the stock for consideration to the group. They may choose to use the *Stock Selection Guide* which contains evaluation methods developed and provided by NAIC (National Association of Investors Corporation). In every issue of the NAIC *Better Investing* magazine, a company is profiled using the *Stock Selection Guide*. If you want to join an existing club in your area or if you want to start an investment club, the NAIC is a good place to start.

Additional Resources for Investment Clubs

American Association of
Individual Investors (AAII)
625 North Michigan Avenue
Chicago, IL 60611
Phone: 312-280-0170
Toll-free: 1-800-428-2244
<www.aaii.org>

National Association of Investors
Corporation (NAIC)
P.O. Box 220
Royal Oak, MI 48068
Phone: 248-583-6242
Toll-free: 1-877-275-6242
<www.better-investing.org>

NAIC Youth Membership Department
P.O. Box 220
Royal Oak, MI 48068

Stock Selection Guide© 1996 by NAIC

Stock Selection Guide Tutorial
(Internet)
Investment Club Central
<www.iclubcentral.com/ssg/>

U.S. Securities and Exchange
Commission (SEC)
Toll-free: 1-800-SEC-0330
<www.sec.gov>

Value Line Investment Survey
220 East 42nd Street
New York, NY 10017
Phone: 212-907-1500
Toll-free: 1-800-634-3583
<www.valueline.com>

The Wall Street Journal
200 Liberty Street
New York, NY
Toll-free: 1-800-975-8609
<www.wsj.com>

SECURITIES AND EXCHANGE COMMISSION (SEC)
The federal agency created by the Securities Exchange Act of 1934 to administer that act and the Securities Act of 1933. The statutes administered by the SEC are designed to promote full public disclosure and protect the investing public against fraudulent and manipulative practices in the securities markets.

Investing Resources on the Internet

The computer databases and information for investment decisions are no longer reserved for big institutional investors. The Internet has dramatically changed investing by opening Wall Street to every individual investor with a computer and a modem. Currently, more people trade securities online than purchase books, CDs, or other products online. Online trading is estimated to have doubled in 1998 and almost doubled again between 1999 and 2000. By the year 2002, more than 20% of American households will invest electronically. (For information on Internet fraud, see Unit 11.)

Several things make the Internet appealing to investors. Once you have the hardware, software, and modem connection, the cost of getting information is low. In fact, many of the financial newspapers, magazines, and financial network sites are free. Depending on how elaborate and detailed the information you want, you can get lots of free information and some information for minimum monthly fees.

Advantages of Investing Resources Online

Going to the Internet for investing information is appealing because you are in control. The Internet is very hands-on. If you want to be actively involved, just point and click. Internet investing is also very private and can be done at home anytime. You can do many different kinds of financial transactions on the Internet. You can buy and sell stocks, bonds, and mutual funds as well as find the best rates on insurance, mortgages, credit cards, and airline tickets. The list of items you can buy and sell on the Internet is growing all the time. You can move money from one bank account to another, you can check on the value of your portfolio, and you can get an instant report on a hot new company. By eliminating the salesperson, the broker, or the financial adviser, you've also accepted all the risks of the investment decision.

What kind of investing help is available on the Internet? First, printed information in the form of magazines and periodicals is present in cyberspace, including major publications such as:

+ Dow Jones' *Wall Street Journal*
+ *Fortune* magazine
+ *Investor's Business Daily*
+ McGraw-Hill's *Business Week*
+ *Smart Money* Magazine
+ Time Warner's *Money* magazine

Newswire services and television broadcasters are also delivering investing information online.

The Internet is not necessarily a passive medium. You can receive personalized updates about investments and have business and industry news sent to you automatically—weekly, daily, or several times a day depending on your interests and needs.

Through the Internet, you can find out what other investors are doing. Too busy to join a club but want to ask questions or "listen" to conversations of other investors? You can do that through organized e-mail sessions called "chat rooms" and discussion forums.

The Internet can aid the individual investor or investment club in the decision-making process. You can study stocks and mutual funds, read annual reports, and obtain stock quotes—available free through many sites. You can also set up a portfolio of investments you own or are "watching."

Disadvantages of Investing Resources Online

There are also disadvantages of online investing resources. The ease of the Internet can be a burden. Unless you resist the addictive nature of trading activity, you can find yourself trading simply because you can, rather than because you should. Investment discipline is an issue. To avoid the pitfall of the easy trade, a sound financial strategy is more important than ever.

News via the Internet reaches everyone very swiftly. But that urge to act on the financial news, or "hot tips," gets many investors in trouble. Research shows that among buyers of more volatile stocks, those who ignored the news earned more than twice as much as news junkies.

Research in the *Quarterly Journal of Economics* published in 1997 compared investors who watched stock funds monthly and those who checked once a year. The monthly watchers concentrated on interim volatility and moved money into lower-earning bond funds, whereas the yearly group stuck with the stock fund and ended up with twice as much money. The more you check your investments, the more they'll seem to bounce up and down. Remember, investing is a long-term proposition. You don't have to watch the market and your investments every day. And don't rush to buy a stock "in the news" on the Internet.

"**Churning**" is a term for turnover of your portfolio. Individuals should beware of investment professionals who are constantly selling and buying investments within a portfolio—churning to make money on **commissions**. But when you are in charge of your own portfolio, you can also be susceptible to selling and buying too frequently. By forgetting your long term strategy, you, too, will be guilty of wasting money on commissions—even if online commissions are low. Some individual investors have reported increasing their trades from six a month to 60 a month. Don't let this happen to you.

CHURNING
When a broker excessively trades an account for the purpose of increasing his or her commissions, rather than to further the customer's investment goals.

COMMISSION
Fees paid to a broker for executing a trade based on the number of shares traded or the dollar amount of the trade.

Investing Online: Choosing an Internet Brokerage Firm----

A number of brokerage services have started online trading services. Some are new companies established for Internet trading only, while others are the newest offering in service from some long-standing brokerage firms. The major issues in choosing an online broker are **cost, access, service, and support.** Whichever you choose to use, there are several criteria you might consider before you actually "trade" online.

> Features to look for are:
> + Low commissions + Available technical support
> + Low monthly fees + Variety of products and research links
> + Free and unlimited real-time quotes + 24-hour access to place trades

Online brokerage firms may advertise a low-cost online trade, but be sure to investigate all the costs. Some firms charge a flat fee plus some pennies, for example two cents, per share traded. Another firm may charge a low fee for a **market order** but more for an odd lot order (a round lot is an even multiple of 100 shares, anything else is an "odd" lot). Some firms charge an "activity fee" that is assessed on an annual basis. This fee is charged to account holders who are less active than others. Be sure to see how you fit that definition or ask to get the fee waived.

Some brokerage firms offer special offers for investment clubs that establish an account with them and trade the club's investments through the online broker. Other brokerage firms charge clubs a per-month charge for **real-time quotes.** Be sure to read the fine print before your club chooses one online broker over another.

What about online security, an issue most commonly mentioned by people new to online investing? The first issue is protection. What will you do if your online broker goes out of business? Most brokers have Securities Investor Protection Corporation (SIPC) account insurance of $500,000 as a base amount. Many firms add secondary coverage, raising the protection to millions of dollars. The second issue is online security of the financial transactions. The computer software referred to as a browser is the system that allows you to navigate the Internet. Online security is accomplished by **encryption**, or coding, that occurs between the browser and the Internet site. Encryption makes it nearly impossible for someone to enter unauthorized trades or observe your account details on the Internet. Some online brokers offer **dual password access**, meaning that the partners in the investment club, for example, can view the online account and investments and use the brokerage resources. A second password is required for actually executing a buy or sell order.

How to Get Started Investing on the Internet----------------

To get started investing online, go to the online investor Web sites and take a "test drive" or a demonstration, which you'll find on most of the Web sites. After you've selected the online broker of your choice, you'll need to complete an account application. You can do this by completing the online application form or by printing the form, filling it in, signing it, and mailing it with a check. The minimum to open

MARKET ORDER
An order to buy or sell a stated amount of a security at the best possible price at the time the order is received in the marketplace.
REAL-TIME QUOTES
A requirement that Market Makers report each trade in a NASDAQ security to NASDAQ within 90 seconds of execution. The information is current up to 90 seconds of the market, as opposed to more typical quotes that are delayed 15 or 20 minutes of the market activity.

Notes

an account is usually between $1,000 and $15,000. An online application may speed up the process of opening your account but will require you to fund the account with your credit card, not a debit card. You will be notified by e-mail when your account is established and you may begin placing buy and sell orders online.

Summary

Whether online trading appeals to you may depend upon how you choose to use your time. You may decide you don't have the time or that you don't have the expertise to do your own investing. That's why some people still go to brokers and financial planners; they'd rather let someone else worry about how the stock market is doing, give them advice, and hold their hand. The choice is up to you.

Resources

The following lists contain more resources to help you with investment decisions.

Books

Barron's Guide to Making Investment Decisions (1998) by Douglas Sease and John A. Prestbo, Prentice Hall.

Buying Stock Without a Broker (1996) by Charles B. Carlson, McGraw-Hill.

Dictionary of Finance and Investment (1998) John Downes and Jordan E. Goodman, Barrons Educational Series.

Free-Lunch on Wall Street (1993) by Charles Carlson, McGraw-Hill.

Investing Online (1997) by Stephen Eckett, published by Financial Times-Putman.

Investing Online for Dummies, 2nd Edition (1998) by Kathleen Sindell, IDG Books Worldwide.

Making the Most of Your Money (1997) by Jane Bryant Quinn, Simon & Schuster.

The Motley Fool Investment Guide (1997) by David Gardner and Tom Gardner, Fireside.

The Motley Fool: Investment Workbook (1998) by David Gardner and Tom Gardner, Fireside.

No-Load Stocks (1997) by Charles Carlson, McGraw-Hill.

Starting and Running a Profitable Investment Club (1998) by Thomas E. O'Hara, Times Books.

The Worth Guide to Electronic Investing (1996) by Jim Jubak, Harper Collins.

WSJ Guide to Understanding Money and Investing (1994) by Kenneth Morris, et al., Simon & Schuster.

Newsletters and Home Study

DRIP Investor (monthly newsletter about Dividend Reinvestment Plans) North Star Financial, Inc.
7412 Calumet Avenue • Hammond, IN 46324-2692
Phone: 219-931-6480
<www.dripinvestor.com>

Disclaimers

The content of this publication is believed to be current as of this printing, but subsequent legislative and regulatory changes and new developments may date the material.

Mention of a trademark, proprietary product, or commercial firm in text or figures does not constitute an endorsement by the Cooperative Extension System or the publisher and does not imply approval to the exclusion of other suitable products or firms.

Investment Home Study
American Association of Individual Investors
625 North Michigan Avenue, Suite 1900 • Chicago, IL 60611
<www.aaii.org> (see web site for free Investor Update e-mail newsletter)
Phone: 1-800-428-2244

The Moneypaper (monthly stock newsletter)
555 Theodore Fremd Avenue, Suite B-103 • Rye, NY 10580
<www.directinvesting.com/moneypaper>
Phone: 1-800-388-9993

Magazines

Better Investing (NAIC)	*Kiplinger's Personal Finance*	*Smart Money*
Consumer Reports	*Money*	*Worth*
Forbes	*Mutual Funds*	

Web Resources

All addresses begin with the http:// prefix.

Daily Financial Updates

BusinessWeek Online <www.businessweek.com/investor/index.html>
CNNmoney <money.cnn.com>
InfoGate (download this software for personal stock updates)
    <www.infogate.com>
MSN Money <moneycentral.msn.com>
Quicken <www.quicken.com/investments>
Silicon Investor (a one-time membership fee is required) < www.techstocks.com>
The Street (by subscription) <www.thestreet.com>
USA Today Money Section <www.usatoday.com/money>
The Wall Street Journal <www.wsj.com>

Investing—General

Alliance for Investor Education: The Investors Clearinghouse
    <www.investoreducation.org>
American Association of Individual Investors <www.aaii.org>
American Stock Exchange <www.amex.com>
Briefing offers in-depth analyses of individual stock sectors <www.briefing.com>
DailyStocks <www.dailystocks.com>
Dow Jones Industrial Average <www.djindexes.com>
GreenMoney online guide for socially responsible investing and green consumer
    options <www.greenmoney.com>
ICLUB Central <www.iclub.com>
Initial Public Offerings at IPO Maven <www.123jump.com/ipomaven.htm>
Investing Online Resource Center (maintained by the North American Securities Administrators Association) <www.investingonline.org>

Investor Protection Trust <www.investorprotection.org>
Investors' Law Center for individuals abused through investing
    <www.investoraid.com>
The Motley Fool, online financial forum <www.fool.com>
NASAA (North American Securities Administrators Association)
    to look up State Securities Regulators <www.nasaa.org>
NASD (National Association of Securities Dealers, Inc.) Individual Investor
    Services <investor.nasd.com>
Nasdaq® <www.nasdaq.com>
National Association of Investors Corporation <www.better-investing.org>
New York Stock Exchange <www.nyse.com>
PC Quote <www.pcquote.com>
Research magazine <www.researchmag.com>
SEC's EDGAR Database for company annual reports and other documents
    <www.sec.gov/edgar.shtml>
SEC's Enforcement Complaint Center <www.sec.gov/complaint.shtml>
SEC's Office of Investor Education and Assistance <www.sec.gov/investor.shtml>
Security Dealers' Public Disclosure site to check if your broker has had any
    disciplinary action filed <www.nasdr.com/2000.asp>
The Stock Room <www.stockroom.org>
Stock Smart <www.stocksmart.com>
StockScreener <www.hoovers.com> (click on IPO Central, then StockScreener)
U.S. Securities and Exhange Commission (SEC) maintains a database on mutual
    fund prospectuses and annual reports <www.sec.gov>

Investing—Mutual Funds

Investment Company Institute <www.ici.org>
Lipper Analytical Services <www.lipperweb.com>
Morningstar Mutual Funds <www.morningstar.com>
Mutual Funds Interactive <www.brill.com>
Mututal Funds Investor Center <www.mfea.com>
Mutual Funds Magazine online <www.mutual-funds.com>

Online Brokers

Accutrade, Inc. <www.accutrade.com>
American Express <www.americanexpress.com> (click on Financial Services)
Ameritrade <www.ameritrade.com>
Ameritrade Plus <www.ameritradeplus.com>
Datek Online <www.datek.com>
CSFB Direct <www.csfbdirect.com>
E*Trade <www.etrade.com>
Fidelity <www.fidelity.com>
Morgan Stanley Online <www.online.msdw.com>
Quick & Reilly <www.quickandreilly.com>
Charles Schwab & Co. <www.schwab.com>
Waterhouse Securities <www.waterhouse.com>

Action Steps

✔ Take action now.

Getting Help: Investing Resources

Check off the steps after you have completed them.

❑ Begin by reading the business and financial pages in the newspaper on a regular basis.

❑ Subscribe to a personal finance magazine.

❑ Find out if an investment club meets in your area and visit one of their meetings.

❑ Read business and finance news on the Internet: Visit *USA Today* Money page <www.usatoday.com/money>; *The Wall Street Journal* <www.wsj.com>; or Quicken <www.quicken.com> investments.

❑ Read a business or finance magazine on the Internet: *Money* magazine <money.cnn.com> or *Smart Money* <www.smartmoney.com>.

❑ Investigate mutual fund information online: *Morningstar* is the leading provider of mutual fund statistics and analysis <www.morningstar.com> or Mutual Fund Education Alliance <www.mfea.com> or Lipper Analytical Services <www.lipperweb.com>.

❑ Set up a "portfolio" online of stocks you own or are watching.

❑ Research a company or an industry online. Request that information, such as the Annual Report, be sent to you in the mail or by e-mail. Search SEC's EDGAR database for information about the company.

❑ Go to the library and see if *Value Line Investment Survey* is available. Review the information on how to read *Value Line* pages and look up a company you are interested in knowing more about.

Author Profile

Linda Kirk Fox, Ph.D., is currently the Director of the School of Family & Consumer Sciences at the University of Idaho, Moscow. She recently served as the state specialist in family economics at the University of Idaho, Moscow. Dr. Fox has developed educational programs and materials including the award-winning *Enhancing the Financial Literacy for Older Youth* videoconference and the Idaho Financial Literacy Coalition. Her University of Idaho Cooperative Extension publications include *Making Financial Decisions When Divorce Occurs* and *Estate Planning: An Idaho Guide*.

Selecting Your Team of FINANCIAL PROFESSIONALS

— Jane Schuchardt, Ph.D., USDA Cooperative State Research, Education, and Extension Service—

Being an investor takes some know-how. You can do it yourself using the investing resources discussed in Unit 9. Or you can reach out to people in the financial services industry to find the advice you need. This unit will help you decide if you need professional help and, if so, where to find it and how to make good choices. A single professional probably cannot provide all the help you'll need. This unit will help you build a team of financial professionals.

Getting financial help is a little like building a house. Most often, it takes a whole team of people to get the job done—a plumber, electrician, carpenter, carpet layer, roofer, and more. To get your financial house in order also takes a team of professionals—banker, tax preparer, attorney, insurance agent, employee benefit counselor at your place of work, stock broker, and financial planner. You need to know when to use which professional, if at all, and for what purpose. As a beginning investor, the human resources consultant at your place of work may help you make investment decisions regarding your retirement plan. Stock brokers and financial planners are most likely to provide investment advice and recommend products. Insurance agents provide access to investment products through cash value life policies. Some banks also sell investments.

The bottom line is the financial services industry is complex and becoming more so every day. But don't let this hold you back. Plenty of information is available to help you make your decisions (see Unit 9), as are many wise and trustworthy advisors who can help you through the complexities.

Investing on Your Own

There is absolutely nothing wrong with going it alone as a beginning investor. Being self-educated reduces your dependence on others for advice. Further, it creates a situation where you can grow in knowledge and confidence as your investments grow in value. To help you educate yourself, we will discuss where to obtain information and how to sort through the extensive material available.

Sources of Information

Beyond this home study course, there are many sources of information for the beginning investor that range from free to quite costly. Here are some places to start:

> ✓ Your local public library investment reference section
> ✓ The World Wide Web (see Unit 9, Getting Help: Investor Resources)
> ✓ Your local bookstore
> ✓ Newspapers, magazines, and other periodicals
> ✓ Pamphlets, workshops, and other educational materials provided by the Cooperative Extension System (CES), a public-funded, nonformal educational system. County Extension offices are conveniently located in courthouses, post offices, or other government buildings. To find a state or county Extension office, visit the Web site of the federal partner, USDA Cooperative State Research, Education, and Extension Service at <www.reeusda.gov> and click on State Partners.

Sorting Through Information Overload

The toughest thing about personal financial management information, especially investments, is dealing with the mass of information that's available. How do you sort the good from the bad? How do you find good resources that can guide you in making decisions? How can you avoid the "hard sell" and truly find good consumer information and not a so-called "education resource" that is really marketing a product or service.

Contacting your Cooperative Extension office or the U.S. Securities and Exchange Commission (SEC) can put you in touch with unbiased, basic investor information. Signing up for this home study course, and seeing it through completion, is probably the best decision you can make to start you on the road to being an educated investor.

Use caution when using business-sponsored materials. Be sure the resource is solely educational, not designed to blatantly or subliminally sell a product or service. A true educational resource does not contain the business sponsor's brand name, trademark, related trade names, or corporate identification in the text or illustrations.

> In addition, information you can trust needs to be:
> ✓ Complete. Materials may mislead by omission. If you're not familiar with a subject, it is difficult to tell what has been omitted. It is important, therefore, to refer to several sources, making sure that you consult at least one reference from a source that you know is unbiased, such as the Cooperative Extension System or the SEC.
> ✓ Objective and unbiased. Differing points of view are given.
> ✓ Accurate. Information can be verified easily. Statements mirror established fact.
> ✓ Understandable. Technical terms are used sparingly and are fully defined.

Investing For Your Future

Getting Help

You may not have the confidence, time, or motivation to wade through stacks of information to make investment decisions. Creating your team of financial professionals and establishing a trusting relationship with each of them can reap significant benefits. This section will get you started and help you make wise investment choices.

Why, When, and How Often?

Financial advisors can save you time. All of us would like to put our hard-earned money to work making more money. But searching through the maze of investment options may take too much of your time. Financial advisors can get specialized information for you quickly. Maybe you've developed a financial plan yourself and want an opinion from someone with more experience than you, or you need to improve your current financial situation and don't know where to start. Financial advisors also are helpful if you have an immediate need or unexpected life event such as a severe illness, birth, death in your family, or an inheritance.

Seeking financial advice is like seeing a physician for your health. Just as most people need an annual physical exam, at least an annual review of your financial situation, including your investment portfolio, is a good idea. When the markets are showing extreme volatility or you have a significant change in life circumstances (e.g., birth of a child, divorce, severe illness or disability, or death of a spouse), more frequent assessment of your investments is recommended. Just as you call on a physician when you have a particular need, you may also need a financial advisor to help with such issues as tax preparation, buying insurance to protect against catastrophic loss of property, or drawing up a will or trust.

When and how often you seek financial advice really depends on the complexity of your financial situation. The bottom line is that having someone to call at the right time, for the right purpose, who is familiar with your situation and can lead you to an informed decision, is invaluable.

Members of a Financial Professional Team

Depending on your personal financial situation and how much knowledge you have, your financial professional team can be as large as ten people. Here are the possibilities:

✓ **Bankers** (or their counterparts at credit unions) can help you choose appropriate accounts for your cash and emergency funds.

✓ **Real estate agents** can help you make housing purchase decisions and help you make contact with mortgage lenders. (Note: You can often negotiate a lower sale price by employing a buyer's broker who works for you, not the seller. If the buyer's broker or the broker's firm also lists properties, there may be a conflict of interest, so ask them to tell you if a property is one of their listings.)

✓ **Lawyers** can help you with certain legal implications of your investments, such as real estate or partnerships. They may also provide financial advice, because some are certified financial planners. Choose a lawyer that has the expertise you need (e.g., real estate, family law, estate planning).

✓ **Certified Public Accountants (CPAs) and accountants** (and some highly qualified tax preparers) can answer questions about the income tax consequences of your investments and help you submit your tax return to the Internal Revenue Service. Like lawyers, they may also offer comprehensive financial advice. Many CPAs have a personal finance specialization, designated by the letters PFS. Another recommended tax preparation professional is an Enrolled Agent.

✓ **Employee benefit counselors** at your place of work can help you with decisions related to retirement accounts, if any, available through your employer.

✓ **Life insurance agents** can sell you insurance products (e.g., annuities, whole life insurance, universal life), which have an investment component. Most life insurance agents are trained by the company whose products they sell and may not be knowledgeable about all investment options available to you. Some also may have additional training through the insurance industry and have earned the CLU (Chartered Life Underwriter) designation.

✓ **Estate planners** can help with a strategy for management of your assets at the time of your death. Many estate planners hold the AEP (Accredited Estate Planner) designation, but they are not qualified to prepare legal documents, such as wills, trusts, and powers of attorney. Only a lawyer is qualified for that.

✓ **Investment advisors** (a.k.a., financial consultants) can give you advice on securities (e.g., stocks, bonds) and must be registered with the Securities and Exchange Commission or a state securities agency. The registry designation is RIA (Registered Investment Advisor). Investment advisors cannot sell securities products without a securities license, but being registered does not guarantee competence.

✓ **Stock brokers** may sell you a wide variety of investment products. Large national or regional firms may have special programs for the beginning investor. Brokers may either be full-service or discount. Full-service brokers can provide good financial advice. Discount brokers, who get their name because sales commissions are discounted, sometimes as much as 70%, are useful if you know what you want to purchase. They generally do not offer advice. Stock brokers are licensed by the state(s) in which they buy and sell securities, and they must be registered with a company that is a member of the National Association of Securities Dealers (NASD) and pass NASD-administered securities exams. NASD maintains the Central Registration Depository (CRD), where you can check to see if your broker is registered to sell securities.

✓ **Financial planners** consider your total financial situation to develop a comprehensive plan. This involves taking a "snapshot" of where you are now via a net worth statement, identifying where you want to be financially (e.g, buying a house, financing a child's college education, living comfortably in retirement), and developing recommendations to help close the gap between what you have now and what you need to meet your life's goals. Financial planners look at meeting short- and long-term financial goals and managing risk with insurance, investments, tax planning, retirement planning, and estate planning. Making decisions about one area, such as saving for retirement, has implications for other areas, such as tax planning and investment choices. Working with someone who can give you the complete picture and call on specialized experts (e.g., lawyers, accountants) when needed has its advantages for some people.

Though credentialing for financial planners is not required by federal or state law, it is recommended you seek someone who has met certain standards set by well-recognized organizations. The best known credential is CFP (Certified Financial Planner), which is administered by the Certified Financial Planner Board of Standards in Denver, Colorado (<www.cfp-board.org>). A Chartered Financial Consultant (ChFC) has successfully completed courses from the American College in Bryn Mawr, Pennsylvania. For financial planners who sell or manage assets, being registered with the SEC or the state where they practice is required.

Costs

It is important to be told clearly, and preferably in writing, what the service provided by a financial professional will cost. Generally, payment can be in one of three forms, or a combination.

1. **Salary.** The financial professional gets a paycheck from the company. The company gets the money from fees or commissions charged to you.
2. **Fees.** There may be an hourly rate, a flat rate, a percentage of assets managed by the company, or a percentage of your income. "Fee-only" financial advisors work solely for their clients and are compensated only by a previously agreed upon fee. They do not accept commissions or receive any other compensation for recommending specific products. Many "fee-only" planners are members of the National Association of Personal Financial Advisors. For a list of NAPFA members near you, call 1-888-FEE-ONLY (1-888-333-6659).
3. **Commissions.** These are paid to the financial professional when recommended financial products (e.g., mutual fund) are purchased. Commissions are generally based upon a percentage of the amount you invest in a product.
4. **Combination of fees and commissions.** A financial planner may charge a set fee to develop an investment plan for you and receive commissions from any products purchased to implement the plan.

Notes

Choosing Your Team of Financial Professionals

Choosing your team of financial professionals, and especially those who may advise you on investment decisions, takes some comparison shopping on your part. Say you have decided you could use the help of an investment advisor, a stock broker, or a financial planner. Here's a six-step process that can help you find the financial professional that is best for you.

STEP 1. Get some names.

You can check the yellow pages of your phone book, but a better idea is to work from referrals. Ask your friends, work colleagues, and family members for their recommendations. You can also contact professional organizations for names of professionals practicing in your area. To do this, call toll-free, or check their Web sites.

> American Institute of Certified Public Accountants, Personal Financial Planning Division, 1-888-777-7077 or <www.cpapfs.org>
>
> Financial Planning Association, 1-800-282-PLAN or <www.fpanet.org>
>
> National Association of Personal Financial Advisors, 1-888-FEE-ONLY or <www.napfa.org>
>
> Society of Financial Service Professionals, 1-800-392-6900 or <www.financialpro.org>

STEP 2. Make some calls.

Ask to have information sent to you in writing, including the names of a couple of satisfied clients. You can get a good feel for how a financial professional will work with you by the way that person treats you on the phone and through the mail. Pay special attention to the financial professional's credentials.

STEP 3. Check out references.

Call to see if the person is licensed. For example, all stock brokers must register with National Association of Securities Dealers (NASD) and are listed in the Central Registration Depository (CRD). Call NASD or your state securities regulator to see if the broker is registered, and ask if there are any disciplinary actions on file. Here are some numbers to call to check for disciplinary action taken against a financial professional:

> Certified Financial Planner Board of Standards, 1-888-CFP-MARK
>
> National Association of Insurance Commissioners, 816-842-3600
>
> National Association of Securities Dealers, 1-800-289-9999
>
> North American Securities Administrators Association, 202-737-0900
>
> U.S. Securities and Exchange Commission, 1-800-732-0330

Notes

STEP 4. Set up a face-to-face meeting and ask some questions.

1. How long have you been a financial planner? What other related experience do you have?
2. What are your professional credentials and affiliations?
3. What is your investment philosophy? (You will feel most comfortable with a financial professional whose recommendations are driven by YOUR tolerance for risk and other preferences, not his or hers.)
4. How will we work together (e.g., by phone, electronically, in person) and how frequently?
5. What services do you offer?
6. What can I expect from you?
7. What will it cost and how are you paid?
8. Who will work with me (e.g., the person you are interviewing or a business associate)?
9. May I see a sample financial plan?
10. Are you registered with state or federal regulators?

STEP 5. Ask yourself, "Do I feel comfortable with this person?"

Working with a financial professional making investment decisions requires a relationship of mutual trust and respect. You must feel the financial professional has your best interests in mind and will be responsive to your needs. You must feel completely confident that this person will treat your situation with strictest confidence and act in a professional manner at all times. You must feel that this professional relationship, putting the effects of market volatility aside, will leave you better off than before.

STEP 6. Make the decision.

Ask for a written agreement that details the services to be provided. Demand the best. Keep up your end of the relationship by providing prompt and accurate information about your current financial situation, your short- and long-term financial goals, and your tolerance for investment risk. Advisors are required by law to make recommendations that are suitable for you; so they need to know a lot about you and your objectives.

Summary

Selecting your team of financial professionals, and especially someone to advise you on investments, is only the first step. Building this relationship and getting the most payback for your investment dollar requires constant monitoring on your part. Be involved. Ask questions. Review your portfolio periodically, at least yearly, to be sure your investment strategy will help you reach your financial goals.

Review monthly statements carefully and understand what they say. Monitor economic conditions (e.g., interest rates) to see things on the horizon that may affect your investments. Then consult with your financial professional for advice. If you have a problem or complaint about your financial professional, act quickly to resolve the situation (see Unit 11 for how to complain).

Building your financial professional team is only a start. Being an active part of that team will increase your chances of making wise investment choices. Often, financial professionals stay with you for a lifetime and can be as great an asset as a solid net worth. Choose wisely.

Work on the Action Steps now to get started.

Action Steps

✓ Take action now.

Selecting Your Team of Financial Professionals

Check off the steps after you have completed them.

❑ Resolve to develop a financial plan to guide your investment choices.

❑ Read at least one financial planning resource and decide if you can prepare and execute a plan yourself.

❑ List your financial goals using the "$MART Financial Goal-Setting" worksheet in Unit 1 on page 9. Determine which goals, if any, require professional help to achieve.

❑ Match the financial goal with the professional best suited to help you achieve the goal.

❑ Use the six-step plan given under "Choosing Your Team of Financial Professionals" in this Unit to select the right professional for you.

❑ Become familiar with a couple of resources on investing and consult them often.

❑ Stay involved in the process—stay educated enough about the topic to ask hard questions, closely monitor the professional's work, and balance your trust in the professional with a healthy amount of consumer skepticism.

References and Resources

North American Securities Administrators Association (NASAA)
10 G Street NE, Suite 710
Washington, DC 20002
Phone: 202-737-0900
<www.nasaa.org>

U.S. Securities and Exchange Commission
Office of Investor Education and Assistance
450 Fifth Street NW, Mail Stop 2-13
Washington, DC 20549-0213
Toll-free information line: 1-800-732-0330
Phone: 202-942-7040
Fax: 202-942-9634
E-mail: help@sec.gov

66 Ways to Save Money—by the Consumer Literacy Consortium, single copies available for 50 cents each from Save Money, Pueblo, CO 81009. Make your check or money order payable to Superintendent of Documents. Or read it on the Web at <www.ftc.gov/bcp/conline/pubs/general/66ways/index.html>.

What You Should Know About Financial Planning and *10 Questions to Ask When Choosing a Financial Planner*—pamphlets available at no charge from the CFP Board of Standards. Call toll-free at 1-888-237-6275, or visit the Web site at <www.cfp-board.org>.

When and How to Choose a Financial Planner—pamphlet available at no charge from the National Endowment for Financial Education. For a free copy, send a stamped, self-addressed envelope to National Endowment for Financial Education, 5299 DTC Boulevard, Suite 1300, Greenwood Village, CO 80111. Visit their Web site at <www.nefe.org>.

Author Profile

Jane Schuchardt, Ph.D., is National Program Leader, USDA Cooperative State Research, Education, and Extension Service, Washington, DC, the federal partner in the Cooperative Extension System. During 1999, she was Senior Fellow with the National Endowment for Financial Education, Denver.

Investment FRAUD

Katherine Philipp, U.S. Securities and Exchange Commission

I nformation is an investor's best tool when it comes to investing wisely and avoiding fraud. And the best way to gather information is to *ask questions*— about both the investment and the person or firm selling it. It doesn't matter if you are a beginner or have been investing for many years, it's never too early or too late to start asking questions.

Too many investors who've suffered losses at the hands of swindlers could have avoided trouble if they had only asked basic questions from the start. One simple phone call—to your state securities regulator or the U.S. Securities and Exchange Commission (SEC)—can often make the difference between investing in a legitimate business or squandering your money on a scam.

This unit will help you recognize and avoid different types of investment fraud. You'll also learn what questions to ask before investing, where to get information about companies, who to call for help, and what to do if you run into trouble.

Navigating the Investing Frontier: Where the Frauds Are

Many fraudsters rely on the telephone to carry out their investment scams. Using a technique known as **cold calling** (so-called because a caller telephones a person with whom they have not had previous contact), these fraudsters will hound you to buy stocks in small, unknown companies that are highly risky or, sometimes, part of a scam. In recent years, the Internet has also become increasingly attractive to fraudsters, because it allows an individual or company to communicate with a large audience without spending a lot of time, effort, or money.

You should be skeptical of any offers you learn about from a cold caller or through the Internet. Here's what you need to know about cold calling and Internet fraud.

Cold Calling

For many businesses, including securities firms, cold calling serves as a legitimate way to reach potential customers. Honest brokers use cold calling to find clients for the long term. They ask questions to understand your financial situation and investment goals *before* recommending that you buy anything.

Dishonest brokers use cold calling to find "quick hits." Some set up "boiler rooms" where high-pressure salespeople use banks of telephones to call as many potential investors as possible. Aggressive cold callers speak from persuasive scripts that include retorts for your every objection. As long as you stay on the phone, they'll keep trying to sell. And they won't let you get a word in edgewise.

Whether the calls are annoying, abusive, or downright crooked, you *can* stop cold callers. The law protects you by requiring cold callers to follow several rules.

When people from the securities industry call to sell something, they must:

◆ **Call Only Between 8:00 A.M. and 9:00 P.M.** These time restrictions do not apply if you are already a customer of the firm or you've given them permission to call you at other times. Cold callers may call you at work at any time.

◆ **Say Who's Calling and Why** Cold callers must promptly tell you their name; their firm's name, address, and telephone number; and that the purpose of the call is to sell you an investment.

◆ **Put You on Their "Do-Not-Call" List, If You Ask** Every securities firm must keep a "do-not-call" list. If you want to stop sales calls from a firm, tell the caller to put your name and telephone number on the firm's "do-not-call" list. If anyone from that firm calls you again, get the caller's name and telephone number, note the date and time of the call, and complain to the firm's compliance officer, the SEC, and your state securities regulator. At the end of this unit, you'll find information on how to make a complaint.

◆ **Treat You With Respect** Cold callers can't threaten or intimidate you or use obscene or profane language. They also can't call you repeatedly to annoy, abuse, or harass you.

◆ **Get Your Written Approval Before Taking Money Directly from Your Bank Accounts** Before investing, you should always get answers to the questions below and written information about an investment. If you do decide to buy from a cold caller, do not give your checking or savings account numbers to the broker over the phone. Brokers must get your written permission—such as your signature on a check or an authorization form—before they can take money from your checking or savings account.

◆ **Tell You the Truth** People selling securities must tell you the truth. Brokers who lie to you about any important aspect of an investment opportunity violate federal and state securities laws.

To learn more about how to deal with cold calls, how to stop them, and how to evaluate any investment opportunity that comes your way over the telephone, read the SEC's *Cold Calling Alert*. You'll find this brochure on the SEC's Web site at <www.sec.gov/investor/pubs/coldcall.htm>, or you can order it by calling the SEC's toll-free publications line at 1-800-SEC-0330.

Internet Fraud

The Internet serves as an excellent tool for investors, allowing them to easily and inexpensively research investment opportunities. But the Internet is also an excellent tool for fraudsters. That's why you should always think twice *before* you invest your money in any opportunity you learn about through the Internet.

Anyone can reach tens of thousands of people by building an Internet Web site, posting a message on an online message board, entering a discussion in a live "chat" room, or sending mass e-mails. It's easy for fraudsters to make their messages look real and credible. But it's nearly impossible for investors to tell the difference between fact and fiction.

> The most common methods for Internet investment scams are:
>
> ◆ **Online Investment Newsletters** Hundreds of online investment newsletters have appeared on the Internet in recent years. Many offer investors seemingly unbiased information free of charge about featured companies or recommend "stock picks of the month." While legitimate online newsletters can help investors gather valuable information, some online newsletters are tools for fraud. Some companies pay cash or securities to people who write online newsletters in exchange for recommending their stocks. While touting isn't illegal by itself, the federal securities laws require the newsletters to disclose who paid them, the amount, and the type of payment. But many fraudsters fail to do so. Instead, they'll lie about the payments they received, their independence, their so-called research, and their track records. These fraudsters usually stand to profit handsomely if they convince investors to buy or sell particular stocks.
>
> ◆ **Online Message Boards** Online message boards, whether newsgroups, Usenet, or Web-based bulletin boards, are an increasingly popular forum for investors to share information. Bulletin boards typically feature "threads" of messages on various investment opportunities. While some messages may be true, many are bogus—or even scams. Fraudsters often pump up a company or pretend to reveal "inside" information about upcoming announcements, new products, or lucrative contracts. Also, you never know for certain who you're dealing with—or whether they're credible—because many bulletin boards allow users to hide their identity behind multiple aliases. People claiming to be unbiased observers who've carefully researched the company may actually be company insiders, large shareholders, or paid promoters. A single person can easily create the illusion of widespread interest in a small, thinly traded stock by posting a series of messages under various aliases.
>
> ◆ **E-mail Spams** "Spam" (junk e-mail) is so cheap and easy to create that fraudsters increasingly use it to find investors for bogus investment schemes or to spread false information about a company. Many more potential investors can be targeted with spam than with cold calling or mass mailing. Using a bulk e-mail program, spammers can send personalized messages to thousands and even millions of Internet users at a time.

Notes

Notes

For more information about how to protect yourself from Internet fraud, visit the SEC's Web site at <www.sec.gov/investor/pubs/cyberfraud.htm>. If you're considering investing online, read the SEC's online investing tips at <www.sec.gov/investor/pubs/onlinetips.htm>.

Types of Investment Fraud

The types of investment fraud seen online mirror the frauds perpetrated over the phone or through the mail. Here are the most common investment schemes and the "red flags" you should watch for:

The "Pump and Dump" Scam

It's common to see messages posted on the Internet that urge readers to buy a stock quickly or to sell before the price goes down. Cold callers often call using the same sort of pitch. Often the promoters will claim to have "inside" information about an impending development or an "infallible" combination of economic and stock market data to pick stocks. In reality, they may be insiders or paid promoters who stand to gain by selling their shares after the stock price is pumped up by gullible investors. Once these fraudsters sell their shares and stop hyping the stock, the price typically falls and investors lose their money. Fraudsters frequently use this ploy with small, thinly traded companies because it's easier to manipulate a stock when there's little or no information available about the company.

The Pyramid Scheme

In the classic "pyramid" scheme, participants attempt to make money solely by recruiting new participants into the program. The hallmark of these schemes is the promise of sky-high returns in a short period of time for doing nothing other than handing over your money and getting others to do the same. Money coming in from new recruits is used to pay off early stage investors. But eventually the pyramid will collapse. At some point, the schemes get too big, the promoter cannot raise enough money from new investors to pay earlier investors, and many people lose their money. Figure 1 shows how pyramid schemes can become impossible to sustain.

Figure 1. Pyramid scheme showing number of participants at each level.

Level	Participants	
1	6	
2	36	
3	216	
4	1,296	
5	7,776	
6	46,656	
7	279,936	
8	1,679,616	
9	10,077,696	
10	60,466,176	
11	362,797,056	(greater than U.S. population)
12	2,176,782,336	
13	13,060,694,016	(greater than world population)

Ponzi Schemes

Ponzi schemes are a type of illegal pyramid scheme named for Charles Ponzi, who duped thousands of New England residents into investing in a postage stamp speculation scheme back in the 1920s. Ponzi thought he could take advantage of differences between U.S. and foreign currencies used to buy and sell international mail coupons. Ponzi told investors that he could provide a 40% return in just 90 days compared with 5% for bank savings accounts. Ponzi was deluged with funds from investors, taking in $1 million during one three-hour period—and this was 1921! Though a few early investors were paid off to make the scheme look legitimate, an investigation found that Ponzi had purchased only about $30 worth of the international mail coupons.

Decades later, the Ponzi scheme continues to work on the rob-Peter-to-pay-Paul principle, as money from new investors is used to pay off earlier investors until the whole scheme collapses. In one recent case, a promoter raised more than $45 million from investors in the "Better Life Advertising Pool" during a two-year period, promising to double each investor's money in either 60 or 90 days. Investors were told that their funds would be used to advertise 900-lines and to promote other profit-making business activities. But none of the Club's business activities ever showed a profit. When the SEC obtained a court order freezing the promoter and the Club's assets, the Club owed more than $50 million to investors, yet had only $2.7 million in the bank. Most of the $45 million raised was used to pay off early-stage investors. And the promoter pocketed roughly $1.2 million of investor money, spending the cash on a house, a swimming pool, cars, and other personal items.

Affinity Fraud

"Affinity fraud" describes investment schemes that prey upon members of identifiable groups, including religious communities, the elderly, ethnic groups, and professionals such as lawyers, doctors, or teachers. Fraudsters often exploit the sense of trust and friendship in groups of people who have something in common. For example, in the late 1980s, about 1,000 immigrants from El Salvador saw $6 million of their savings wiped out in a phony investment bank that promoted itself exclusively to Hispanics in the Washington, DC, area.

Fraudsters assume that the tight-knit structure of many groups makes it less likely that a scam will be detected by regulators and law enforcement officials and that victims may be more likely to forgive "one of their own." They'll enlist respected leaders within a community to spread the word about an investment deal. The key to avoid being a victim in an affinity scheme is to ask questions and check out everything—no matter how trustworthy the person is who brings the investment opportunity to your attention.

MICROCAP
The smallest size of company. "Cap" is short for capitalization, which is the share price multiplied by the number of outstanding company shares.

Foreign or "Offshore" Frauds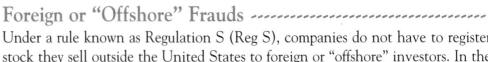

Under a rule known as Regulation S (Reg S), companies do not have to register stock they sell outside the United States to foreign or "offshore" investors. In the typical offshore scam, an unscrupulous **microcap** company sells unregistered Reg S stock at a deep discount to fraudsters posing as foreign investors. These fraudsters then sell the stock to U.S. investors at inflated prices, pocketing huge profits that they share with the microcap company insiders. The flood of unregistered stock into the United States eventually causes the price to plummet, leaving unsuspecting U.S. investors with enormous losses. The SEC recently strengthened Reg S to make these frauds harder to conduct. But you should still be extra careful when considering any investment opportunity that comes from another country, because it's difficult for U.S. law enforcement agencies to investigate and prosecute foreign frauds.

How to Avoid Investment Fraud

To invest wisely and avoid investment scams, research each investment opportunity thoroughly and ask questions. Get the facts *before* you invest, and only invest money you can afford to lose. You can avoid investment scams by asking—and getting answers to—these three simple questions:

1. Is the investment registered?

Many investment scams involve unregistered securities. So you should always find out whether the company has registered its securities with the SEC or your state securities regulators. You can do this by checking the SEC's EDGAR database at <www.sec.gov/edgar.shtml>.

Some smaller companies don't have to register their securities offerings with the SEC, so always check with your state securities regulator. You'll find the number for your state securities regulator in the government section of your phone book. You can also call the North American Securities Administrators Association (NASAA) at 202-737-0900 or visit NASAA's Web site at <www.nasaa.org/nasaa/abtnasaa/ find_regulator.asp>. One simple phone call can make the difference between investing in a legitimate business or squandering your money on a scam.

2. Is the person licensed and law-abiding?

Find out whether the person or firm selling the investment is properly licensed in your state and whether they've had run-ins with regulators or received serious complaints from investors. This information is available from the Central Registration Depository (CRD), a computerized database that contains information about most brokers, some investment advisors, their representatives, and the firms they work for. The CRD also contains information about the broker's educational background and previous employment history.

You can get CRD information from your state securities regulator. Or call the National Association of Securities Dealers Regulation, Inc.'s (NASDR) public disclosure hotline at 1-800-289-9999 or visit their Web site at <www.nasdr.com/2000.asp>. Your state securities regulator may provide more information from the CRD than the NASDR, especially when it comes to investor complaints, so you may want to check with them first.

3. Does the investment sound too good to be true?

If it does, it probably is. High-yield investments tend to involve extremely high risk. Never invest in an opportunity that promises "guaranteed" or "risk-free" returns. Watch out for claims of astronomical yields in a short period of time. Be skeptical of "offshore" or foreign investments. And beware of exotic or unusual-sounding investments. Make sure you fully understand the investment before you part with your hard-earned money. Always ask for—and carefully read—the company's prospectus. You should also read the most recent reports the company has filed with its regulators and pay attention to the company's financial statements, particularly if they do not say they have been audited or certified by an accountant.

The SEC has spelled out all the questions you'll need to ask in the following publications: *Ask Questions*, *Internet Fraud*, and *Microcap Stock*. (The address for obtaining these three is on page 143 under "Pamphlets and Brochures.") When you ask these questions, write down the answers you received and what you decided to do. If something goes wrong, your notes can help to establish what was said. Let your broker or investment advisor know you're taking notes. They'll know you're a serious investor and may tell you more—or give up trying to scam you. The SEC has developed *Form for Taking Notes* to help you. You can get this and other useful publications on the Investor Information section of the SEC's Web site at <www.sec.gov> or by calling 1-800-SEC-0330.

How to Get Information About Companies

Many investment scams involve small microcap companies that don't file reports with the SEC. Professional stock analysts regularly research and write about larger public companies, and it's easy to find their stock prices in the newspaper. In contrast, information about microcap companies can be extremely difficult to find, making them more vulnerable to investment fraud schemes. It's easier for fraudsters to manipulate a stock when there's little or no information available about the company.

If you're working with a broker or an investment advisor you trust, you can ask him or her to get you written information about the company and its business, finances, and management. You can also get information on your own from these sources:

✓ **From the company** Ask the company if it is registered and files reports with the SEC. If the company is small and unknown to most people, you should also call your state securities regulator to get information about the company, its management, and the brokers or promoters who've encouraged you to invest in the company.

✓ **From the SEC** A great many companies must file their reports with the SEC. Using the EDGAR database, you can find out whether a company files with the SEC and get any reports of interest to you. For companies that do not file on EDGAR, contact the SEC's Public Reference Room by calling 202-942-8090, sending a fax to 202-628-9001, or sending an e-mail to publicreference@sec.gov.

✓ **From your state securities regulator** Even though the company does not have to register its securities with the SEC, it may have to register them with your state. Your regulator will tell you whether the company has been legally cleared to sell securities in your state. Contact your state securities regulator to find out whether they have information about the company and the people behind it. Too many investors could easily have avoided heavy and painful financial losses if they had only called their state securities regulator *before* they bought stock. Look in the government section of your phone book or contact NASAA at 202-737-0900 or <www.nasaa.org/nasaa/abtnasaa/find_regulator.asp> to get your state regulator's name and phone number.

✓ **From other government regulators** Many companies, such as banks, do not have to file reports with the SEC. But banks must file updated financial information with their banking regulators, and that information is often available for free on government Web sites. If you have access to the Internet and want to find this information, visit the Federal Reserve System's National Information Center of Banking Information site at <www.ffiec.gov/NIC>, the Office of the Comptroller of the Currency at <www.occ.treas.gov>, or the Federal Deposit Insurance Corporation at <www.fdic.gov>.

✓ **From reference books and commercial databases** Visit your local public library or the nearest law or business school library. You'll find many reference materials containing information about companies. You can also access commercial databases for more information about the company's history, management, products or services, revenues, and credit ratings. Although the SEC cannot recommend or endorse any particular research firm, its personnel, or its products, you may consult a number of commercial resources, including Bloomberg, Dun & Bradstreet, Hoover's Profiles, Lexis-Nexis, and Standard & Poor's Corporate Profiles. Ask your librarian about additional resources.

✓ **The Secretary of State where the company is incorporated** Contact the secretary of state where the company is incorporated to find out whether the company is a corporation in good standing. You may also be able to obtain copies of the company's incorporation papers and any annual reports it files with the state. You'll find the name and address of your state's secretary of state in the government section of your phone book.

> **CAUTION** If you've been asked to invest in a company but you can't find any record that the company has registered its securities with the SEC or your state or any reason to believe that it's exempt from registration, call or write your state's securities regulator or the SEC immediately with all the details. You may have come face-to-face with a scam.

What to Do if You Run into Trouble

Act promptly! By law, you have only a limited time to take legal action. If your problem is with a broker, follow these steps to solve your problem:

1. Talk to your broker and explain the problem. What happened? Who said what, and when? Were communications clear? What did the broker tell you? Did you take notes about what your broker said at the time? If so, what do your notes say?
2. If your broker can't resolve your problem, then talk to the broker's branch manager.
3. If the problem is still not resolved, put your complaint in writing and send it to the compliance department at the firm's main office. Explain your problem clearly, and tell the firm how you want it resolved. Ask the compliance office to respond to you in writing within 30 days.
4. If you're still not satisfied, then send a letter to your state securities regulator or to the Office of Investor Education and Assistance at the SEC along with copies of any letters you've sent already to the firm.

You can get the name, telephone number, and address of your state securities regulator by calling NASAA at 202-737-0900 or by visiting NASAA's Web site at <www.nasaa.org/nasaa/abtnasaa/find_regulator.asp>.

The address for the SEC's Office of Investor Education and Assistance is:

U.S. Securities and Exchange Commission
Office of Investor Education and Assistance
450 Fifth Street NW, Mail Stop 2-13
Washington, DC 20549-0213
Toll-free information line: 1-800-SEC-0330
Phone: 202-942-7040
Fax: 202-942-9634
E-mail: help@sec.gov

To help protect yourself and learn to recognize fraud, follow the action steps at the end of this unit.

Notes

Selected Resources

Video/Other Media --

Investment Scams: What Con Artists Don't Want You to Know.
Investor Protection Trust, 1901 North Fort Myer Drive, Suite 1012-1014, Arlington, VA 22209. <www.investorprotection.org>

Web Sites --

Alliance Against Fraud in Telemarketing—protecting you from fraudulent cold callers <www.fraud.org/aaft/aaftinfo.htm>

Alliance for Investor Education—a coalition of organizations educating investors <www.investoreducation.org>

Investor Protection Trust—state regulators working together to educate investors <www.investorprotection.org>

National Association of Securities Dealers—training and education for individual investors <www.investor.nasd.com>

National Association of Securities Dealers Regulation—check out your broker's background <www.nasdr.com>

National Fraud Information Center—Web site and toll-free number (800-876-7060) to report fraud <www.fraud.org>

National Futures Association—for experienced investors to learn more about commodities <www.nfa.futures.org>

National Institute for Consumer Education—curriculum on the *Basics of Investing* <www.nice.emich.edu>

North American Securities Administrators Association—find your state securities regulator <www.nasaa.org/nasaa/abtnasaa/find_regulator.asp>

Office of Investor Education and Assistance, U.S. Securities and Exchange Commission <www.sec.gov/investor.shtml>

U.S. Consumer Gateway—links to government Web sites for consumers <www.consumer.gov>

Pamphlets and Brochures

Ask Questions
Cold Calling Alert
Financial Facts Tool Kit
Internet Fraud
Microcap Stock
How to Avoid Ponzi and Pyramid Schemes

U.S. Securities and Exchange Commission
450 Fifth Street NW, Mail Stop 2-13
Washington, DC 20549-0213
For a complete list, see <www.sec.gov/answers.shtml>

Investment Swindles: How They Work and How to Avoid Them
Investors Bill of Rights
Swindlers Are Calling

National Futures Association
200 West Madison Street
Chicago, IL 60606
<www.nfa.futures.org>

Affinity Fraud: Beware of Swindlers Who Claim Loyalty to Your Group
Field of Schemes: Investment Scams Sprout New Hybrids
How to Spot a Con Artist

North American Securities Administrators Association
10 G Street NE, Suite 710
Washington, DC 20002
<www.nasaa.org/nasaa/scripts/prel_display_list.asp?ptid=63>

Action Steps

✔ Take action now.
Investment Fraud

Check off the steps after you have completed them.

❑ Get a copy of *Form for Taking Notes,* so you remember what questions to ask when someone calls to sell you an investment. The form is available from the SEC at <www.sec.gov/complaint/callform.htm>.

❑ Keep notes of your conversation when you talk to a financial professional who makes recommendations.

❑ To learn more about telemarketing fraud, get a copy of *Swindlers Are Calling,* a publication prepared in cooperation with the Alliance Against Fraud in Telemarketing and distributed by National Futures Association. Also read *Cold Calling Alert* from the SEC at <www.sec.gov/investor/pubs.shtml>.

❑ Download and print out information about investment opportunities you read about online if you think you want to consider investing. If you later decide to invest, you'll have proof of the offer.

❑ Maintain a filing system to keep all confirmation slips, statements, and notes about each investment.

❑ Ask to be put on the "do not call" list if a salesperson's calls are annoying you.

❑ Report any suspicious sales activity to your state securities regulator and to the SEC.

❑ Read *How the SEC Handles your Complaint* at Notes <www.sec.gov/investor/pubs/howoiea.htm>.

❑ Get the name of your state securities regulator at <www.nasaa.org/nasaa/abtnasaa/find_regulator.asp> and put the phone number in a handy place.

❑ Call your state securities regulator and check the CRD for your broker to see if there are any disciplinary problems on file.

❑ Attend an investment seminar sponsored by your local Cooperative Extension office, community college, or adult school.

Author Profile

This unit was written as a cooperative effort of several staff members of the Office of Investor Education and Assistance at the U.S. Securities and Exchange Commission (SEC). The primary author was **Katherine Philipp**, former Investor Education Specialist. Prior to joining the SEC, she was a certified financial planner, a national board member of the National Association of Investors, Inc., and taught personal finance at several colleges in Maryland for 20 years. The Office of Investor Education and Assistance partners with many organizations in their educational programs. Investor protection is the number one goal of the SEC, and the best defense against fraud is an educated consumer. For more information, visit the Web site at <www.sec.gov/investor.shtml>. If you have a complaint or question about your investments, call 1-800-732-0330 or e-mail to help@sec.gov.

Some of the material in this unit is adapted with permission from *The Basics of Saving and Investing*, a teaching guide developed by the National Institute for Consumer Education (NICE) at Eastern Michigan University, <www.nice.emich.edu>. Under an agreement with NICE, the complete curriculum, with units on *Financial Decisions, How Financial Markets Work, Investment Choices, Investment Information*, and *Investment Fraud*, is on the National Association of Securities Dealers (NASD) Web site for individual investors <http://investor.nasd.com/teach/default.html>.

Personal Finance Instructors of America are also using the curriculum with high school students as part of the *Investor Protection Trust's* education campaign with state securities regulators called *Financial Literacy 2010*. For more information about the campaign and high school programs in your state, go to the Web site <www.fl2001.org> or call your state securities regulator.

Action Steps

Summary ✓ Take action NOW.

Unit 1: Basic Building Blocks of Successful Financial Management

☐ Reduce expenditures to free up money to achieve financial goals.

☐ Compare financial account statements provided by institutions with personal records.

☐ Complete an annual financial checkup, including net worth and cash flow statements.

☐ Build a team of financial advisors to guide and direct financial decision making.

☐ Review financial management strategies periodically and revise when necessary.

☐ Determine/establish an adequate amount of emergency fund for your individual situation.

☐ Deposit funds in easily available accounts where they can be accessed with minimal financial penalties.

☐ Locate your insurance policies such as life, health, property, casualty, automobile, and disability.

☐ Evaluate current insurance policies and shop around for additional or replacement coverage, if indicated.

☐ Learn about tax laws and use related strategies to reduce total taxes owed.

☐ Check your income tax withholding level and adjust, if indicated.

☐ Explore the advantages of different tax strategies.

☐ Use tax-advantaged and tax-deferred options when appropriate, i.e., IRAs, 401(k), 403(b).

☐ Maximize tax deductions (e.g., using home equity credit lines versus nondeductible consumer interest).

☐ Write out short-, medium-, and long-term goals following the $MART goal format (see pages 5–9).

☐ Keep credit use at a safe, manageable level.

☐ Obtain a copy of your credit report to see if it is accurate and complete.

☐ Establish and periodically evaluate wills and estate plans.

Unit 2: Investing Basics

☐ Review where you are currently holding money, and determine if your holdings are in savings or investment vehicles.

☐ Determine the rate of return for current financial holdings.

☐ Complete the "What Are Your Investment Preferences?" exercise (see page 21) to identify your characteristics and needs as an investor.

❏ Set aside time each week to read one of the personal finance magazines recommended in Unit 9.

❏ Assess your interest, skill, and time to make decisions about your investment plan and portfolio.

❏ Proceed on your own or seek assistance.

Unit 3: Finding Money to Invest

❏ Develop a plan to ensure that you save the money needed to fund your goals.

❏ Set up a regular savings program, if you do not already have one.

❏ Identify two strategies you could implement to help you accumulate funds to invest.

❏ Identify a money-consuming habit that you would be willing to change.

❏ Calculate the amount of money you can realize in one year by changing this habit.

❏ Change your behavior, save the appropriate amount of money, and invest it.

❏ Track your investment and watch it grow.

Units 4 and 5: Ownership and Fixed-Income Investing

❏ Read about equity and fixed-income investments in "the financial press."

❏ Investigate equity and fixed-income investments available through your employer plan, if available.

❏ Obtain additional investment information from Cooperative Extension or financial services firms.

❏ Identify equity and fixed-income investments that match your goals and available cash flow.

❏ Research these investments and compare at least three specific products (e.g., stocks).

❏ Calculate the percentage of your portfolio allocated to equity and fixed-income investments.

❏ Determine your marginal tax bracket (see Unit 7) to see if tax-exempt investments such as municipal bonds are cost-effective.

Unit 6: Mutual Fund Investing

❏ Investigate mutual fund investment choices (e.g., stock funds) available through your employer plan.

❏ Decide upon your selection criteria (e.g., minimum deposit, low expense ratio).

❏ Identify specific mutual funds that match your investment goals.

❏ Call at least three mutual fund firms for a prospectus.

❏ Do further reading on those mutual funds and mutual funds in general (e.g., prospectus, books).

❏ Do follow-up research using Morningstar or Value Line.

- [ ] Complete a mutual fund application and make an investment.
- [ ] Track the progress of your funds at least quarterly.

Unit 7: Tax-Deferred Investing

- [ ] Inquire if your employer has a tax-deferred retirement plan [e.g., 401(k)].
- [ ] Find out what investment choices are available within the employer plan.
- [ ] Find out if your employer matches your investment dollars and if so, by how much.
- [ ] Set a date to start contributing or to increase your contribution—either a dollar amount or a percentage of your salary.
- [ ] If you are self-employed, determine the type of retirement plan you could start, set an amount to save, and begin making contributions.
- [ ] Investigate IRAs and determine which is best for your age and income level.
- [ ] Increase contributions to your tax-deferred plan each time your pay increases.

Unit 8: Investing With Small Dollar Amounts

- [ ] Investigate inexpensive investment options available through your employer, if available [e.g., 401(k) and savings bond purchase plans].
- [ ] Attend an employer-sponsored investment seminar.
- [ ] Identify at least three "shoestring" investments that match your goals and available cash flow.
- [ ] Research these investments and compare at least three specific products (e.g., three large company growth funds). Use the "Shoestring Investment Comparison Worksheet" (see page 109) to record the key features of each.
- [ ] Dollar-cost average mutual fund purchases and/or enroll in an automatic investment program.
- [ ] Investigate the initial minimum deposits required for specific investments and ways that they can be reduced (e.g., automatic investment plan).

Unit 9: Getting Help: Investing Resources

- [ ] Start reading the business and financial pages in the newspaper on a regular basis.
- [ ] Subscribe to a personal finance magazine.
- [ ] Find out if an investment club meets in your area and ask to visit one of their meetings.
- [ ] Read business and finance news on the Internet at Web sites <www.usatoday.com/money>, <www.wsj.com>, and <www.quicken.com/investments>.
- [ ] Read a business or finance magazine on the Internet (e.g., <www.smartmoney.com>).

☐ Investigate mutual fund information online at Web sites <www.morningstar.com>, <www.mfea.com>, and <www.lipperweb.com>.

☐ Set up a "portfolio" online of stocks you own or are watching.

☐ Research a company or industry online (e.g., search the SEC's EDGAR database).

Unit 10: Selecting Your Team of Financial Professionals

☐ Develop a financial plan to guide your investment choices.

☐ Read at least one financial planning resource and decide if you can prepare and execute a plan yourself.

☐ Match your financial goals with the professional advisor best suited to help you achieve them (e.g., lawyer, financial planner).

☐ Use the six-step plan described under "Choosing Your Team of Financial Professionals" on page 128 to select the right professional for you.

☐ Become familiar with resources on investing and consult them often.

☐ Stay involved in the process—stay educated enough about investing to ask hard questions and closely monitor a professional's work. Balance your trust in a professional with a healthy amount of consumer skepticism.

Unit 11: Investment Fraud

☐ To help you remember what questions to ask when someone calls to sell you an investment, get a copy of a form for taking notes from the SEC Web site <www.sec.gov/complaint/callform.htm>.

☐ Keep notes of your conversation with a financial professional who makes recommendations.

☐ To learn more about telemarketing fraud, get a copy of *Swindlers Are Calling* from the National Futures Association <www.nfa.futures.org/investor/SAC.html>. Also read *Cold Calling Alert* from the SEC <www.sec.gov/investor/pubs.shtml>.

☐ Download and print out information about investment opportunities you read about online if you think you want to consider investing. If you later decide to invest, you'll have proof of the offer.

☐ Maintain a filing system to keep all confirmation slips, statements, and notes about each investment.

☐ Ask to be put on the "do not call" list if a salesperson's calls are annoying you.

☐ Report any suspicious sales activity to your state securities regulator and to the SEC.

☐ Read *How the SEC Handles Your Complaint or Inquiry* at <www.sec.gov/investor/pubs/howoiea.htm>.

☐ Get the name of your state securities regulator from <www.nasaa.org/nasaa/abtnasaa/find_regulator.asp> and put the phone number in a handy place.

☐ Call your state securities regulator and check the central registration depository (CRD) file for your broker to see if there are any disciplinary problems on file.

Glossary of Investment Terms

12b-1 Fee: A marketing fee levied on mutual fund shareholders to pay for advertising and distribution costs, as well as broker compensation.

401(k) Plan: A retirement savings plan, generally sponsored by private corporations, that allows an employee to contribute pretax dollars to a company investment vehicle until the employee retires or leaves the company.

403(b) Plan: Similar to a 401(k), a retirement savings plan for employees of a tax-exempt education or research organization or public school. Pretax dollars are contributed to an investment pool until the employee retires or terminates employment.

Annual Report: A report that public companies are required to file annually that describes the preceding year's financial results and plans for the upcoming year. Annual reports include information about a company's assets, liabilities, earnings, profits, and other year-end statistics.

Annuity: A contract by which an insurance company agrees to make regular payments to someone for life or for a fixed period in exchange for a lump sum or periodic deposits.

Asset Allocation: The placement of a certain percentage of investment capital within different types of assets (e.g., 50% in stock, 30% in bonds, and 20% in cash).

Asset Allocation Fund: Mutual fund that holds varying percentages of stock, bonds, and cash within its portfolio.

Automatic Investment Plan: An arrangement where investors agree to have money automatically withdrawn from a bank account on a regular basis to purchase stock or mutual fund shares.

Automatic Reinvestment: An option available to stock and mutual fund investors where fund dividends and capital gains distributions are automatically reinvested to buy additional shares and thereby increase holdings.

Balanced Fund: Mutual fund that holds bonds and/or preferred stock in a certain proportion to common stock in order to obtain both current income and long-term growth of principal.

Bear Market: Term used to describe a prolonged period of declining stock prices.

Before (Pre) Tax Dollars: Money contributed to a tax-deferred savings plan that you do not have to pay income tax on until withdrawal at a future date.

Beta: A measure of a stock's volatility; the average beta for all stocks is +1.

Blue-Chip Stock: Term, derived from the most expensive chips in a poker game, to indicate the stock of companies with long records of growth and profitability.

Bond: A debt instrument or IOU issued by corporations or units of government.

Bond Fund: Mutual fund that holds mainly municipal, corporate, and/or government bonds.

Broker: A professional who transfers investors' orders to buy and sell securities to the market and generally provides some financial advice.

Bull Market: Term used to describe a prolonged period of rising stock prices.

Buy and Hold: A strategy of purchasing an investment and keeping it for a number of years.

Capital Appreciation: An increase in market value of an investment (e.g., stock).

Capital Gains Distribution: Payment to investors of profits realized upon the sale of securities.

Capitalization: The market value of a company, calculated by multiplying the number of shares outstanding by the price per share. Capitalization is often called "cap" for short in the names of specific investments (e.g., ABC Small Cap Growth Fund).

Cash-Value Life Insurance: Type of life insurance contract that pays benefits upon the death of the insured and also has a savings element that builds cash value prior to death.

Central Registration Depository (CRD): A computerized system that includes the employment, qualification, and disciplinary histories of more than 400,000 securities professionals who deal with the public. Consumers can get CRD information about a sales representative by calling 1-800-289-9999 or visiting the Web site <www.nasdr.com/2000.htm>.

Certificate of Deposit (CD): An insured bank product that pays a fixed rate of interest (e.g., 5%) for a specified period of time.

Churning: Excessive trading of securities within an account by a broker for the purpose of increasing his or her commissions, rather than to further a client's investment goals.

Class A Shares: Mutual fund shares that incur a front-end sales charge upon purchase.

Class B Shares: Mutual fund shares that incur a back-end sales charge (also known as a contingent deferred sales charge or CDSC) if sold within five to six years of purchase.

Class C Shares: Mutual fund shares that incur higher management and marketing fees than Classes A and B, but no sales or redemption charges upon purchase or sale.

Closed-End Fund: An investment company that issues a limited number of shares that can be bought and sold on market exchanges.

Cold Calling: A practice used by salespeople of making unsolicited phone calls to people they don't know in order to attract new business.

Collectible: An investment in tangible items such as coins, stamps, art, antiques, and autographs.

Commission: Fee paid to a broker to trade securities, generally based on the number of shares traded (e.g., 100 shares) or the dollar amount of the trade.

Commodities: An investment in a contract to buy or sell products such as fuel oil, pork, grain, coffee, sugar, and other consumer staple items by a specified future date.

Common Stock: Securities that represent a unit of ownership in a corporation.

Composite Indices: Stock market indices comprised of stocks traded on major stock exchanges:
  New York Stock Exchange Composite (index of stocks traded on New York Stock Exchange)
  American Stock Exchange Composite (index of stocks traded on American Stock Exchange)
  NASDAQ Composite (index of stocks traded over-the-counter in the quotation system of the National Association of Securities Dealers).

Compound Interest: Interest credited daily, monthly, quarterly, semiannually, or annually on both principal and previously credited interest.

Convertible Securities: Bonds or preferred stock that can be exchanged for a fixed number of shares of common stock in the same corporation.

Core Holding: The foundation of a portfolio (e.g., a stock index fund) to which an investor might add additional securities.

Corporate Bonds: Debt instruments issued by for-profit corporations.

Direct Purchase Plans (DPPs): "No load" stocks where every share, including the first, can be purchased directly from a company without a broker.

Discount Broker: A broker that trades securities for a lower commission than a full-service broker.

Diversification: The policy of spreading assets among different investments to reduce the risk of a decline in the overall portfolio from a decline in any one investment.

Dividend: A distribution of income from investments to shareholders.

Dividend Reinvestment Plans (DRIPs): Plans that allow investors to automatically reinvest any dividends a stock pays into additional shares.

Dollar-Cost Averaging: Investing equal amounts of money (e.g., $50) at a regular time interval (e.g., quarterly) regardless of whether securities markets are moving up or down. This practice reduces average share costs to investors, who acquire more shares in periods of lower securities prices and fewer shares in periods of higher prices.

Dow Jones Industrial Average: The most widely used gauge of stock market performance. Also known as "The Dow," it tracks 30 stocks in large well-established U.S. companies.

EDGAR (Electronic Data Gathering, Analysis, and Retrieval): An electronic system developed by the U.S. Securities and Exchange Commission (SEC) that is used by companies to file documents required by the SEC for securities offerings and ongoing disclosure. EDGAR information is available to consumers on the Internet at <www.sec.gov>, usually within 24 hours after filing by a company. EDGAR information is also available in the SEC's public reference room by calling (202) 942-8090 or sending a fax to (202) 628-9001 or an e-mail to publicreference@sec.gov.

Equity Investing: Becoming an owner or partial owner of a company or a piece of property through the purchase of investments such as stock, growth mutual funds, and real estate.

Federal Deposit Insurance Corporation (FDIC): Federal agency that insures bank deposits up to $100,000. Investments purchased at banks are not FDIC-insured.

Fixed Annuity: An investment vehicle, often used for retirement accounts, that guarantees principal and a specified interest rate. Fixed annuity earnings grow tax-deferred until withdrawal.

Full-Service Broker: A broker that charges commissions based on the type and amount of securities traded. Full-service brokers typically charge more than discount brokers but also provide more extensive services (e.g., research and personalized advice).

GNMAs or Ginnie Maes: An investment in a pool of mortgage securities backed by the Government National Mortgage Association (GNMA).

Growth Fund: Mutual fund that invests in stocks exhibiting potential for capital appreciation.

Growth Stocks: Stock of companies that are expected to increase in value.

Guaranteed Investment Contract (GIC): Fixed-income investments offered in many tax-deferred employer retirement plans that guarantee a specific rate of return for a specific time period.

Income Fund: Mutual fund that invests in stocks or bonds with a high potential for current income, either interest or dividends.

Income Stocks: Stock of companies that expect to pay regular and relatively high (compared to growth stocks) dividends.

Index: An unmanaged collection of securities whose overall performance is used as an indication of stock market trends. An example of an index is the widely quoted Dow Jones Industrial Average, which tracks the performance of 30 large company U.S. stocks.

Index Fund: Mutual fund that attempts to match the performance of a specified stock or bond market index by purchasing some or all of the securities that comprise the index.

Individual Retirement Account (IRA): A retirement savings plan that allows individuals to save for retirement on a tax-deferred basis. The amount of savings that is tax deductible varies according to an individual's access to pension coverage, income tax filing status, household income, and the type of IRA that is selected.

Interest Rate Risk: The risk that, as interest rates rise, the value of previously issued bonds will fall, resulting in a loss if they are sold prior to maturity.

Investment Clubs: Organizations of investors who meet and contribute money regularly toward the purchase of securities.

Investment-Grade Bond: Bond rated with one of the top four grades by a rating service like Moody's and Standard & Poor's, indicating a high level of creditworthiness.

Investment Objective: The goal (e.g., current income) of an investor or a mutual fund. Mutual fund objectives must be clearly stated in their prospectus.

Keogh Plan: A qualified retirement plan for self-employed individuals and their employees to which tax-deductible contributions up to a specified yearly limit can be made if the plan meets certain requirements of the Internal Revenue Code.

Limit Order: An order to buy or sell securities that specifies that a trade should be made only at a certain price or better.

Liquidity: The quality of an asset that permits it to be converted quickly into cash without a loss of value.

Load: A commission charged by the sponsor of a mutual fund upon the purchase or sale of shares.

Management Fee: The amount paid by mutual funds to their investment advisors.

Marginal Tax Rate: The rate you pay on the last (highest) dollar of personal or household (if married) earnings.

Market Order: An order to buy or sell a stated amount (e.g., 100 shares) of a security at the best possible price at the time the order is received in the marketplace.

Market Value: The current price of an asset, as indicated by the most recent price at which it traded on the open market. If the most recent trade in ABC stock was at $25, for example, the market value of the stock is $25.

Maturity: The date on which the principal amount of a bond, investment contract, or loan must be repaid.

Microcap Stock: Low-priced stocks issued by the smallest of companies. Companies with low or "micro" capitalization typically have limited assets and a small total market value. Many microcap stocks trade in small volumes in the "over-the-counter" (OTC) market, with prices quoted on the OTC Bulletin Board or "Pink Sheets." For more information about microcap stocks, check the Web site <www.sec.gov/investor/pubs/microcapstock.htm>.

Money Market Mutual Fund: A highly liquid mutual fund that invests in short-term obligations such as commercial paper (corporate IOUs), government securities, and certificates of deposit.

Moody's Investors Service: A rating agency that analyzes the credit quality of bonds and other securities.

Mutual Fund: An investment company that pools money from shareholders and invests in a variety of securities, including stocks, bonds, and money market securities.

Net Asset Value (NAV): The market value of a mutual fund's total assets, after deducting liabilities, divided by the number of shares outstanding.

Net Worth: The dollar value remaining when liabilities (what you owe) are subtracted from assets (what you own). Example: $200,000 of assets – $125,000 of debt = $75,000 net worth.

Online Investing: The purchase of securities from brokerage firms via the Internet using a computer and modem.

Open-End Fund: An investment company that continually buys and sells shares to meet investor demand. It can have an unlimited number of investors or money in the fund.

Penny Stocks: Stocks that sell for $5 per share or less.

Portfolio: The combined holding of stocks, bonds, cash equivalents, or other assets by an individual or household, investment club, or institutional investor (e.g., mutual fund).

Preferred Stock: A type of stock that offers no ownership or voting rights and generally pays a fixed dividend to investors.

Price/Earnings (P/E) Ratio: The price of a stock divided by its earnings per share (e.g., $40 stock price divided by $2 of earnings per share = a P/E ratio of 20).

Principal: The original amount of money invested or borrowed, excluding any interest or dividends.

Prospectus: An official booklet that describes a mutual fund. It contains information as required by the U.S. Securities and Exchange Commission on topics such as the fund's investment objectives, investment restrictions, purchase and redemption policies, fees, and performance history.

Real Estate: Land, permanent structures on land, and accompanying rights and privileges, such as crop or mineral rights.

Real Estate Investment Trust (REIT): A portfolio of real estate–related securities in which investors can purchase shares that trade on major stock exchanges.

Real-Time Quotes: A requirement that trades in a NASDAQ (over-the-counter market) security be reported within 90 seconds of execution. Thus, information is current up to 90 seconds of the market, rather than typical quotes which have a 15- or 20-minute delay.

Reciprocal Immunity: A principle of taxation where state and local governments don't tax earnings on federal debt securities and the federal government doesn't tax earnings on state/local debt securities.

Risk: Exposure to loss.

Risk Management: Actions taken (e.g., purchase of insurance) to provide protection against catastrophic financial losses (e.g., disability and liability). Risk management is an important investing prerequisite.

Sales Charge: The amount charged to purchase mutual fund shares. The charge is added to the net asset value per share to determine the per share offering price.

Savings Incentive Match Plan for Employees (SIMPLE Plan): A tax-deferred retirement plan for owners and employees of small businesses that provides matching funds by the employer.

Securities: A term used to refer to stocks and bonds in general.

Securities and Exchange Commission (SEC): Federal agency created to administer the Securities Act of 1933. Statutes administered by the SEC are designed to promote full public disclosure about investments and protect the investing public against fraudulent and manipulative practices in the securities markets.

Securities Investor Protection Corporation (SIPC): A nonprofit corporation that insures investors against the failure of brokerage firms, similar to the way that the Federal Deposit Insurance Corporation (FDIC) insures bank deposits. Coverage is limited to a maximum of $500,000 per account, but only up to $100,000 in cash. SIPC does not insure against market risk, however.

Simplified Employee Pension (SEP): A tax-deferred retirement plan for owners of small businesses and the self-employed.

Standard & Poor's 500 Index: An index that is widely replicated by stock index mutual funds. Also known as the S&P 500, it consists of 500 of the largest U.S. companies.

Standard & Poor's Corporation: A rating agency that analyzes the credit quality of bonds and other securities.

Stock: Security that represents a unit of ownership in a corporation.

Substandard Grade ("Junk") Bond: Bond rated below the top four grades by a rating service such as Moody's and Standard & Poor's. They generally provide a higher return than investment-grade securities to compensate investors for an increased risk of default.

Tax Deferral: Investments where taxes due on the amount invested and/or its earnings are postponed until funds are withdrawn, usually at retirement.

Tax-Exempt: Investments (e.g., interest from municipal bonds) where earnings are free from tax liability.

Total Return: The return on an investment including all current income (interest and dividends), plus any change (gain or loss) in the value of the asset.

Treasuries: Debt obligations of the U.S. government secured by its full faith and credit and issued at various schedules and maturities.

Unit Investment Trust (UIT): An unmanaged portfolio of professionally selected securities that are held for a specified period of time.

U.S. Treasury Securities: Debt instruments issued by the federal government with various maturities (bills, notes, and bonds).

Value Stock: A stock with a relatively low price compared to its historical earnings and the value of the issuing company's assets.

Variable Annuity: An annuity where the value fluctuates based on the market performance of its underlying securities portfolio.

Volatility: The degree of price fluctuation associated with a given investment, interest rate, or market index. The more price fluctuation that is experienced, the greater the volatility.

Zero-Coupon Bonds: Debt instruments issued by government or corporations at a steep discount from face value. Interest accrues each year but is not paid out until maturity.

About NRAES

NRAES, the Natural Resource, Agriculture, and Engineering Service (formerly the Northeast Regional Agricultural Engineering Service), is a land grant university outreach program focused on delivering educational materials and training opportunities in support of cooperative extension. The mission of NRAES is to assist faculty and staff at member land grant universities in increasing the public availability of research- and experience-based knowledge. All NRAES activities are guided by faculty from member land grant universities (see the map below for a list of cooperating members).

NRAES began in 1974 through an agreement among the cooperative extension programs in the Northeast. The program is guided by the NRAES Committee, which consists of a representative from each member university, the NRAES director, and an administrative liaison appointed by the Northeast Cooperative Extension Directors Committee.

Currently, NRAES has published more than 100 books and distributes more than 180 on topics such as general agriculture, fruit and vegetable production, perennials production, integrated crop management, greenhouse, and composting. For more information and a free catalog, contact NRAES.

Natural Resource, Agriculture, and Engineering Service (NRAES)
Cooperative Extension
152 Riley-Robb Hall
Ithaca, New York 14853-5701

Phone: (607) 255-7654
Fax: (607) 254-8770
E-mail: NRAES@CORNELL.EDU
Web site: WWW.NRAES.ORG

Marty Sailus, NRAES Director
Jeff Popow, Managing Editor

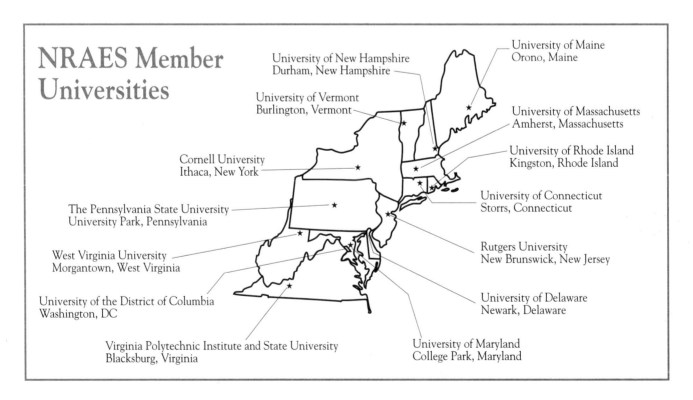

NRAES Member Universities

University of New Hampshire
Durham, New Hampshire

University of Maine
Orono, Maine

University of Vermont
Burlington, Vermont

University of Massachusetts
Amherst, Massachusetts

Cornell University
Ithaca, New York

University of Rhode Island
Kingston, Rhode Island

The Pennsylvania State University
University Park, Pennsylvania

University of Connecticut
Storrs, Connecticut

West Virginia University
Morgantown, West Virginia

Rutgers University
New Brunswick, New Jersey

University of the District of Columbia
Washington, DC

University of Delaware
Newark, Delaware

Virginia Polytechnic Institute and State University
Blacksburg, Virginia

University of Maryland
College Park, Maryland